The
Pocket Guide to
ENGLISH
WORDS

Terry Freedman
and
Iseabail Macleod

RICHARD DREW PUBLISHING
Glasgow

© Terry Freedman and Iseabail Macleod

First published 1987
by Richard Drew Publishing Limited
6 Clairmont Gardens
Glasgow G3 7LW, Scotland

Designed by James W. Murray

British Library Cataloguing in Publication Data

Macleod, Iseabail
Pocket guide to English words.
1. English language ——— Glossaries,
vocabularies, etc.
I. Title
428.1   PE1680

ISBN 0-86267-192-2

Set in Scantext Clearface by John Swain Ltd Glasgow
Printed and bound in Great Britain by Cox & Wyman Ltd

PREFACE

by Dr Nigel Vincent, Department of Linguistics,
University of Cambridge

MANY PEOPLE are plagued by doubts about spelling and vocabulary, grammar and style. Others believe firmly in the rules they were forced to learn at school and set their faces against new usages and recent idiom. Both share the belief that the right answers to questions about language exist in the kinds of reference book we call grammars and dictionaries. And of course in one sense they are right. It is always convenient and reassuring to be able to find what one is looking for written down in black and white. Yet in another important sense they are wrong, for grammars and dictionaries exist to record usage, not to determine it.

Keeping track of usage in an increasingly complex world is not, however, easy and modern dictionaries and grammars tend to be of forbidding size and complexity. The present compilation therefore provides an invaluable service. It offers help and advice, it comments and explains, all with admirable clarity and restraint. It strikes a nicely-judged balance between newly-established spellings and usages — such as recognising that computer buffs fill their *disks* with *programs* while DJs fill their *programmes* with *discs* — and hardy perennials, such as the disentanglement of pairs like *infer/imply* or *disinterested/uninterested*. Most important of all, perhaps, it suggests a model we can all follow; it shows us how to take responsibility for solving our own linguistic problems by paying careful attention to current usage.

Nigel Vincent
Cambridge
1987

INTRODUCTION

Most of us have at some time had embarrassing
doubts about certain aspects of the English language.
The *Pocket Guide to English Words* is an alphabeti-
cal list of words which often cause problems of spelling,
meaning, pronunciation or usage, together with examples of how to use them. It includes groups of words
which are easily confused, such as *its/it's*, *affect/effect*,
words which are too new to be found in ordinary
dictionaries, such as *Aids*, *GCSE*, many computer
terms, common abbreviations and various points of
difficulty which people often hesitate or argue over,
such as *if I were you/if I was you*. Commonly used
terms in grammar and punctuation are illustrated with
examples to show them in use.

It can be vitally important to write in a presentable form
such things as formal letters, job applications, a
curriculum vitae. This little book gives numerous and
varied examples of these and other forms of written
English which can be used as models.

We have used the word 'acceptable' rather than
'correct' in many cases when recommending that a
particular word or structure can be used, because
correct English is, in the end, only what the majority of
English speakers actually use and accept as clear,
understandable and up-to-date.

A

a/an: the indefinite article: **an** is used before: **1** a vowel: *an apple*. **2** silent *h: heir, honour, hour, honest*. Note that the *h* in hotel and historian is usually pronounced nowadays and it is commoner to say: *a hotel, a historian*.

AA Automobile Association; Alcoholics Anonymous.

abbreviations full stops at the end of abbreviated words are no longer always considered necessary, especially where the terms are in frequent use eg *Mr, Mrs, Dr, BBC, TUC, MOT*. However, some people still prefer a full stop at the end of an abbreviation which does not end in the original final letter: *no.* (number), *co.* (company). See also **apostrophe** and **north.**

abbr., abbrev. abbreviated: abbreviation.

-able/-ible There is no rule as to when an adjective is formed by adding **-able** or **-ible**, though **-ible** is less common. Words which form adjectives with **-able** usually drop final *e* (*advisable*). Exceptions are verbs ending in *-ce* (*noticeable*) and *-ge* (*changeable*) and a small number of one-syllable verbs, eg like (*likeable*).

aborigines/aboriginal: aborigines pronounced [aboridgineez] is the usual name given to the people who have lived in a country, especially Australia, since early times: *Captain Cook found Australia inhabited* *by aborigines.* The singular **aborigine** is only used in informal speech and it is more correct to use **aboriginal**: *He is an aboriginal.* Also used as an adjective: *aboriginal customs.*

abortion/miscarriage both refer to the birth of a baby at such an early stage that it does not live. In non-medical language, **abortion** usually refers to a case where this is caused deliberately and **miscarriage** where it is accidental: *The Catholic Church is against abortion. She has had three miscarriages but still hopes to have a child.*

abstract *adjective* pronounced [**abstract**] referring to things of the mind rather than material objects: *abstract ideas.* **abstract art** made up of shapes and colours rather than recognizable things.

noun pronounced [**abstract**] **1** a summary of a report, article etc, especially a scientific one: *They publish abstracts of chemical journals.* **2** a piece of abstract art: *When Picasso first painted abstracts, people complained that the pictures did not represent anything.*

verb pronounced [ab**stract**] **1** a formal word, to remove something from something else: *They abstract sugar from the cane.* **2** used humorously to mean to steal. **3** to make a shortened version of: *All these articles have been abstracted from Physics Today.*

a/c account.

academic 1 concerned with learning or belonging to a place of learning: *The academic staff of the institute* *includes part-time as well as full-time teachers.* **2** theoretical and unlikely to be put into practice: *a purely academic argument.* **3** too intellectual to be useful in a practical situation: *This academic approach to the Third World will not produce food for starving children.*

accent/dialect: accent means the system of pronunciation which is typical of a certain region or group of people: *Some Londoners have a Cockney accent.* **dialect** means a form of the language that is spoken in a certain region or by a particular group of people. It is different from the standard language of the country not only in pronunciation, but in words and the way they are used: *A dialect speaker in the North-West of England might say 'Give us a butty' when he wants a jam sandwich.* See also **standard English**.

accessary/accessory both are correct, but **accessary** is less common except in legal language: *By giving the burglar a key, he became an accessary to the crime.*

accommodation note the spelling.

account 1 a description of something: *She gave a clear account of her experiences.* **2 accounts** a record of money paid into or out of a company or other organization: *Their accounts are made up every January.* **3** a way of keeping money in a bank or other financial organization. There are different kinds of account:

current account an account from which one can withdraw money at any time, but which normally gives no interest on the money in it. See **cheque, bank card** and **cash card** (under **credit card**).

deposit account an account which gives interest on the money in it if it is left there for a certain time. Sometimes it is necessary to give a certain amount of notice before money can be withdrawn.

savings account a kind of deposit account where the interest rate is sometimes higher and usually the time required to withdraw money is longer. See also **credit account**.

4 account/bill/invoice are all documents showing how much a customer owes: **account** a list of the goods or services supplied with the dates and charges, the amounts paid and still owing and the balance the customer still has to pay. **bill** a written or printed statement of what is owed by a customer, usually with little or no detail. **invoice** a list of goods or services supplied to a customer together with the charges; sometimes the customer is asked to regard this as a bill: 'Please pay on receipt of invoice' is often written on an invoice.

acknowledgement note the spelling: *I received no acknowledgement to my long letter to the Manager apart from a brief phone call from his secretary.*

acoustic note the spelling: *The new roof in the concert hall is causing acoustic problems because the sound of the orchestra seems to be muffled.* See also **-ics**.

acquiesce note the spelling; to agree to something.

When asked to visit the hospital Princess Margaret graciously acquiesced.

acquaint note the spelling: *I am not acquainted with 1920s jazz.*

acquire note the spelling: *When asked how he had acquired the video recorder, James said he had got it for his birthday.*

acquit note the spelling: *The magistrate decided to acquit the boy because he did not seem to know that he had committed a crime.*

acronym a series of initials used as an abbreviation for several words and pronounced as one word: *BASIC (Beginners' All-purpose Symbolic Instruction Code).*

acrostic the term used when the first or last letters of each line of a crossword or poem combine to make a word:

POP
ARE
NET

Act of Parliament see **Bill**.

actually often condemned as overused and empty of meaning. However, used sparingly it is an acceptable and useful way of opening a conversation and giving the speaker time to think: *Actually Ben is coming today if he can get a lift.*

acute *noun* a mark placed above a vowel to show pronunciation, eg in French: *café.*

acute/chronic Both words refer to a bad condition or illness but **acute** refers to a sudden crisis in need of urgent attention: *After tasting the mushrooms he collapsed with acute stomach pains.* **chronic** is used of a longstanding illness or problem which is hard to cure: *chronic bronchitis. Chronic unemployment in the area is partly the result of industrial decline.*

adapter/adaptor: adapter a person who alters something to make it suitable for a different use, especially a book, play or musical work: *She was employed as an adapter of classical novels for very young children.*

　adaptor an electrical fitting which allows one kind of plug to be used with a different type of socket.

　However, it is now common to find either of these spellings used for either meaning.

AD abbreviation for *anno domini* (Latin, meaning in the year of Our Lord) to indicate the number of years after the birth of Christ: *Augustus died in AD 14.* Compare **BC**.

ad see **advertisement**.

address see **letters**.

adherence/adhesion: 1 only **adhesion** sticking firmly to something: *When the glue has been left to harden all night adhesion will be complete.* **2 adhesion** or **adherence** following a political or religious belief or other cause with strictness and loyalty: *He was known for his adhesion to the anti-apartheid movement.*

adjacent/adjoining: adjacent describes something that is next to or bordering another thing or place: *Although our garden is adjacent to the park, we have no access.* **adjoining** describes somewhere physically connected to another place with access from one to the other: *I like a bedroom with an adjoining bathroom.*

adjective a word which describes a noun: a *black* pen; a *large* dog.

Special forms are used when comparing something (or someone) with another or others. To form a **comparative adjective**, usually *-er* is added: Max is small*er* than Ben. When singling out one from a group (a **superlative adjective**), *-est* is usually added: Max is the small*est* in the class.

Some adjectives, especially longer words, use *more* or *most* instead of *-er*, *-est*: Cakes are *more* fattening than bread. We've just had the *most* wonderful holiday of our lives.

Some words can be used with both forms: Colds are *commoner* (or *more common*) than flu.

adult pronounced [adult].

adult education see **further education**.

adverb a word which gives more information about:
1 a verb: They rushed off *quickly*.
2 an adjective: That's a *very* pretty dress.
3 another adverb: They left *very* quickly the second time.

adverse/averse: adverse a formal word meaning

working against someone's plans etc: *The doctors had some success in treating cholera in spite of adverse conditions in primitive clinics.* **averse** used formally or humorously, followed by **to**, unwilling to accept: *I'm not averse to an occasional drink.*

advertisement pronounced [ad**ver**tisement] Newspapers usually have two types of advertisement:

1 those inserted by companies in order to sell their goods.

2 often known as **classified advertisements**, shortened in informal speech to **ads** or **small ads** inserted by companies or by individuals for various purposes, eg to advertise jobs, sell houses, cars, other things.

If you want to insert an advertisement in a newspaper, it is helpful to make the wording as clear and as short as possible. Note all the important points; for instance when selling something, remember to include the price.

The following is an example of a letter asking a newspaper to insert an advertisement:

4 Martby Road
Warrington
WA2 6EH
27 August 1987

The Weekly Herald
South Street
Northport
SE6 5YJ

Dear Sirs

I should like to insert the following advertisement in *The Weekly Herald* on Friday 1 September:

Three-piece suite for sale. Blue dralon. 5 years old. Excellent condition. £150 ono. Tel. 0583 2747 after 6 pm.

Yours faithfully

Mary Stubbs

Newspapers normally also accept advertisements by telephone.

Replies can be sent to a **box number**, which means that the newspaper will keep them to be collected by the advertiser when convenient. Unless there is some strong reason for this, it is of course simpler and quicker to give a telephone number and/or address.

The following abbreviations are often used in advertisements:

CH   central heating
F/T   full-time
K   1 000
k and b   kitchen and bathroom
ono   or nearest offer
p & p   postage and packing
P/T   part-time
reg or regn   registration (year of a car)
SAE   stamped addressed envelope
SC   self-contained

advice/advise: advice is a noun: *She wrote to a magazine for advice about her dandruff.* **advise** is a verb: *Doctors advise heart patients not to smoke.*

advice note/delivery note: advice note a document sent before a delivery note to tell a customer that the goods he has purchased are on the way; occasionally it accompanies the goods. **delivery note** always accompanies the goods and is usually in duplicate so that the customer can return one signed copy as proof that he has received the goods.

adviser note that the ending is usually *-er*, but *-or* is also acceptable.

advocate see **barrister**.

aerate note the spelling: pronounced [airate]: *The Water Board installed a pump to aerate the river water, because there was not enough oxygen in it.*

aerobics a method of building up physical fitness by doing exercises which improve the rate of a person's consumption of oxygen.

aesthetic/ascetic: aesthetic (also spelt **esthetic**) concerned with standards of beauty especially in the arts and crafts and literature: *The new plastic chairs have no aesthetic appeal, but despite their ugliness, they are comfortable.* **ascetic** avoiding comfort and self-indulgence, usually for religious reasons: *The monks lived an ascetic life with simple food and bare, cold cells.*

affect is a verb meaning to influence or alter: *Premature babies are adversely affected by noise and light.* Note that the corresponding noun is **effect**: *Doctors are studying the effect of noise on young babies.* See also **effect**.

afflict/inflict: afflict usually in the form **afflicted** suffering seriously because of disease, problems etc: *Pity those afflicted with illness and poverty.* **inflict** to cause something to make someone else suffer: *Smokers should not inflict tobacco smells on other people.*

aged pronounced [ayjd] if referring to a particular age: *a boy aged four*, [ayjid] if referring to a very old person: *my aged grandmother*.

ageing note the spelling.

agenda plural **agendas**.

agenda/minutes: agenda, plural **agendas** a list of things to be done or discussed at a meeting, eg of a club or society. This is usually set out in a particular way and circulated amongst the members of the organization in advance or at the start of the meeting.

Example of an agenda:

Wyche Film Society

Meeting to be held at the Badger, Main St, Wyche, on Wednesday 8 June 1988 at 8 pm.

AGENDA

1 Apologies

2 Minutes of 20 May 1988

3 Business arising:
  (a) Festival
  (b) Advertising

4 Financial report

5   Membership committee report

6   Correspondence

7   New business
    (a)   Hiring of hall
    (b)   Programme for meeting August 10
    (c)   Visit of Dr Jens Finke

8   Any other business

9   Date of next meeting

minutes a record of what happened at a meeting based
on notes taken during the meeting by the secretary of
an organization or a committee member who has been
given the task. The draft is usually checked soon after
the meeting with the chairman or someone else present
to ensure that the account is correct. The final version is
often typed and pasted into a special minutes book.

An example of minutes:

Minutes of the meeting of Wyche Film
Society at the Badger, Main St, Wyche on
8 June 1988 at 8 pm.

PRESENT: Dr Andrew Moore, Mrs O Patel,
Dr Damian Simpson, Mr Richard Betteley
and Mrs Barry (Hon Sec).

Apologies for absence: Mr and Mrs S Penn.

MINUTES: The minutes of the meeting held on Wednesday 20 May 1988 were read and approved.

BUSINESS ARISING
1. Festival: The programme drafted by Mrs Patel would be followed, with the addition of a Charlie Chaplin film.
2. Advertising: The Secretary advised that notices in the local press would cost £100. It was agreed that an advertisement be inserted two weeks running in the local papers.

FINANCIAL REPORT: Mr Simpson (Treasurer) presented the financial report which was adopted.

MEMBERSHIP COMMITTEE REPORT: Mrs Patel said that the application of Ray Hollins of Denby Moss, Wyche, had been unanimously approved. Mr Hollins was duly admitted to membership.

NEW BUSINESS
1. Hiring of Goodwill Hall: The Secretary advised that the WI had offered the use of the hall without charge.
2. Programme for next meeting: The Secretary advised that Mr K Nakane had

agreed to show selections from Japanese films.

3. Visit of Prof Finke: Prof Finke had telephoned to say he could give his talk on home horror movies any evening except Sunday. It was agreed to plan for Wednesday and to appoint a sub-committee to consider details of the visit and bring back recommendations to the next meeting. Mrs Barry, Mrs Patel and Dr Moore were appointed to plan this programme.

DATE OF NEXT MEETING: Wednesday 20 August 1988 at 8 pm.

There being no further business the meeting closed at 10 pm.

Confirmed   (Chairman)

Date

Note that for an important decision, a motion may be formally proposed and seconded and recorded as follows:

That membership be restricted to ratepayers of Wyche.

The motion was proposed by Mr Betteley and seconded by Mrs Patel.

aggravate the original meaning is to make worse: *Scratching only aggravates the discomfort caused by itchy chilblains.* However, it is now generally used in informal speech to mean to annoy or irritate: *It aggravates the teacher when Mark gives his homework in late.*

AGM annual general meeting.

agnostic/atheist: an **agnostic** believes that it is impossible to prove or disprove the existence of God; an **atheist** is convinced that God does not exist.

-aholic (based on alcoholic) a part of a word which combines with other words to mean addicted to something: *workaholic.*

AIDS usually now written **Aids**, the abbreviation for *acquired immune deficiency syndrome*, a fatal and increasingly common disease in which the body's defences against infection stop functioning. It is caused by a virus now known as HIV and is spread by dirty hypodermic needles, sexual intercourse with a carrier of the disease and by blood transfusions from infected donors.

ale/beer/bitter/mild/stout: ale formerly the ordinary word for beer, but now used in trade names and also by beer lovers with a taste for 'real ale'. **beer** a drink made of malt, sugar, yeast and hops. **mild** a beer with a light flavour of hops. **bitter** a bitter-tasting beer with a strong flavour of hops. **stout** a strong dark beer flavoured with roasted malt or barley.

A-level until the late 1980s, the advanced level of a

subject taken in the GCE examination, usually two years after the O-level examination. See **GCE** and **O-level**.

alga a very simple water plant, usually used in the plural **algae**, pronounced [aljee] or [algee].

alias/alibi: alias means otherwise known as or named, referring to when a person takes a name which is different from the one he is normally known by: *Ian Smith, alias Fergus Dunn, was caught carrying a stolen passport and large quantities of heroin at Luton Airport.* **alibi 1** the explanation or evidence given by a person accused of a crime to prove that he was somewhere else at the time: *When charged with the Monton burglary, Jane's alibi was that she was in Bolivia at the time.* **2** an excuse: *When you ask him to wash up, his alibi is that he is allergic to washing up liquid.*

allergy having an unusual sensitivity to certain foods, materials or conditions: *The rash may be caused by an allergy.* **allergic** adjective **1** *You may be allergic to wool, strawberries or other fruits, but without doing lots of tests, it is difficult to find the cause of your rash.* **2** used in informal speech to mean disliking something intensely, unable to get on with someone: *I'm allergic to blond men with beards.*

Alliance *see* Liberal.

all right/alright: all right is the correct form; **alright** is widely used but is not yet acceptable in formal writing.

allude to refer to indirectly: *Although the Prime Minister referred to nobody by name, it was clear that she was alluding to the Chief of Police.*

allusion/illusion/delusion: allusion is a passing reference to someone or something: *Ann made no allusion to the fact that Alan was wearing odd socks.* **delusion** and **illusion** are both false beliefs or impressions, but:

delusion is a false impression which is fixed in a person's mind and completely accepted as true: *The patient suffered from the delusion that she was Cleopatra.*

illusion a false impression or belief which is only temporary and which can be replaced later by a true impression, or not believed in at all: *By wearing a black dress and high heels little Dora created an illusion of height and slenderness.*

alternate the adjective is pronounced [ol**ter**nate]: *They went to visit their mother on alternate days.* The verb is pronounced [**ol**ternate]: *They alternated between Blackpool and Scarborough for their holidays.*

alternative *noun* considered by some to refer only to a choice between two things: *Pay the ransom! The alternative is death!* Nowadays it often refers to a wider choice: *He saw two alternatives to marrying Vera: becoming a monk or joining the Foreign Legion.* *adjective* **1** refers to another possible way: *Take the M25 to London or the alternative route through Oxford.* **2** unusual, looked at or done in a different way: *They follow an alternative lifestyle in a* *gypsy caravan*. **alternative medicine** ways of treating illnesses by methods which are different from the normal ones: *In desperation she tried alternative medicine to relieve her pain, including acupuncture and homoeopathy.* See **homeopathy**.

altogether/all together: **altogether** is an adverb meaning in total or completely: *Altogether they had 20 sheep and 20 cows. The weather was altogether too wet for camping.* **all together** means with others at the same time: *They left all together for Paris.*

A.M. or a.m. abbreviation for Latin *ante meridiem*, the period of time between midnight and midday. Compare **P.M.**

amend/emend: **amend** to improve, change or correct: *They have amended the rules of the Jolly Boy Club to allow women to become members.* noun **amendment**.
   emend to correct errors in a book or piece of writing: *The dictionary was emended to remove words considered racist.* noun **emendation**.

amenity pronounced [amenity] or [ameenity] something which makes life more comfortable or pleasant: *Our children are surrounded by sports amenities, including a sports hall, a park and a swimming pool.*

America can refer to: **1** the whole American continent from the north of Canada to Tierra del Fuego in the south; it consists of: **North America** the part to the north of the Isthmus of Panama and **South America**

to the south. The small countries just to the north of the Isthmus are sometimes referred to as **Central America. 2** the **United States of America:** *She lived in America for four years.*

amicable/amiable: amicable friendly: *They have continued to be on amicable terms although they were divorced years ago.* **amiable** pleasant and friendly in temperament: *He has an amiable personality with a jolly manner.*

among/amongst both are correct.

amoral see **immoral**.

amount/number: amount is used of a mass or quantity of something: *Considering the amount of food he eats he is not very fat.* With words which have a plural, number is used: *The number of children who smoke is increasing.* See also **number**.

ampersand the sign meaning and: *Smith & Jones.*

an see **a**.

anagram a word which forms another word if its letters are rearranged: *boy yob.*

anaesthetic/anesthetic both spellings are acceptable, but **anesthetic** is commoner.

analgesic a painkiller.

and is usually used to join two parts of a sentence, but it can sometimes be used at the beginning of the sentence: *Alice loved Wales. And she often thought of her childhood there.*

angry: angry at is used of things and happenings: *He was angry at the slipshod work done by the mechanic.* **angry with** is used for people: *Most of all he was angry with his neighbour who had recommended that garage.*

annex/annexe the verb, meaning to add or join something on, is spelt **annex**: *The enemy tried to annex part of our territory.* The noun, meaning an extra building or an addition to a document, is usually **annexe**, but also **annex**, especially in American English.

annual/perennial: annual 1 once a year: *Many people have their annual holiday in August.* **2** lasting for a year: *The annual subscription to the club is £10.* **3** refers to a plant that completes its life cycle in one year. Also used as a noun: *The border was planted with annuals.* **perennial 1** everlasting. **2** refers to a plant which lasts for several years. Also used as a noun.

anorexia the informal name for **anorexia nervosa** an illness in which a person (usually an adolescent girl) refuses to eat for a long time and loses weight to a dangerous extent. The sufferer has an obsessive wish to lose weight.

antarctic see **arctic**.

ante-/anti- are both used with other words: **ante** means before: *Most hospitals have ante-natal clinics to prepare women for childbirth.* **anti-** means against or opposite: *He is so antisocial that he does not even talk* *to his own family.*

anticipate 1 to expect: *I don't anticipate that they will arrive before us.* Note that some people consider this use of the verb incorrect. **2** to do something earlier, often in order to prevent something else happening: *They had anticipated the trouble in town by sending extra police patrols.*

anyone/anybody both are correct.

apartheid pronounced [apartate] or [apartite]: *In some cities in South Africa apartheid laws mean that a black woman may buy a dress, but cannot use the dressing rooms reserved for white women to try it on.*

apostle/disciple both were followers of Jesus Christ, but **apostle** is the name for any one of the twelve who were chosen to be with him all the time: *Peter and James were two of the apostles.* Note that **disciple** also means the followers of any influential leader.

apostrophe shows: **1** that a letter is missing: *it's* = it is, *don't* = do not; **2** possession: *the dragon's tail* = the tail of the dragon, *the twin's photograph* = the photograph of the twins. However some common singular names ending in *-s* have the apostrophe after the *s: Jesus' mother; Moses' miracles.*

apparatus pronounced [apparaytus].

application for a job see **letters** and **curriculum vitae.**

appro: on appro on approval: *We bought the machine on appro.*

apt to/liable to both mean to have a tendency to do something: *Plastic bags are apt to (liable to) burst if you carry tins and bottles in them.*

Arab/Arabian/Arabic: Arab 1 (of or connected with) a person belonging to a race of people coming originally from certain Middle Eastern countries, eg Saudi Arabia, Lybia, Syria: *Many Arab countries like Saudi Arabia have become prosperous because of their oil.*

Arabian of Arabia, the Arabian Peninsula. It is also used of Arabs in general, but this usage is rather old-fashioned.

Arabic 1 (of) the language of the Arabs. **2** usually **arabic** of numbers written, 1, 2, 3, 4, etc (as opposed to **Roman numerals**, I, II, III, IV).

archaeology or **archeology** both spellings are acceptable.

arctic/antarctic note the spelling; **arctic** describes the region round the North Pole and **antarctic** the region round the South Pole.

arguably fashionable with the meaning perhaps. Do not overuse.

aristocrat pronounced [aristokrat].

array *computers* a group of related pieces of data stored together in the memory of a computer under one label.

arr. arrive(s).

artery/vein: artery the thick tubular muscle which

takes blood away from the heart. **vein** carries blood to the heart.

artist/artiste: artist a person who is skilled in painting, drawing, decoration etc. **artiste** a performer in the theatre, circus or concert hall. **artist** can also be used for this meaning.

as/as if see **like**.

ascetic see **aesthetic**.

asphalt pronounced [asfelt] or [asfolt]: *The local people complained when the playground was paved with asphalt because children used to hurt themselves much less on grass.*

assassinate note the spelling: *The man who tried to assassinate the President said that he wanted to murder everyone in the government.*

assent/consent both mean to agree to something, but **assent** implies passive agreement: *Not knowing the law she assented to the confiscation of her camera.* **consent** is a more conscious decision to say yes: *Her father consented to let Alice marry, although she was only sixteen.*

assertion training a way of teaching people who are easily dominated by others to gain the necessary confidence to deal with other people firmly, but without aggression: *His assertion training gave him the skill to insist on discipline without causing resentment amongst the staff.*

assignation/assignment: assignation a secret

appointment, especially for lovers, to meet: *Romeo and Juliet had an assignation at the friar's cell.*

assignment a special task or project which has been given to someone: *The students had Geography assignments last term.*

ssume/presume both mean to take as a fact without proof but **assume** is less certain: *We will just have to assume that the bill is correct and pay it.* **presume** implies that there is strong evidence: *As you have seven children, I presume you are married.*

ssurance see **insurance**.

sterisk a star-shaped sign in printing or writing used: **1** to indicate a footnote; **2** to show that something is missing: *D*** the government!*

sthma note the spelling; pronounced (**asma**].

stronaut/cosmonaut: astronaut a person specially trained for space travel. **cosmonaut** the Russian term for astronaut.

stronomy/astrology both are subjects involving the stars. **astronomy** is the scientific study of the heavenly bodies. **astrology** is a study not generally considered to be scientific, of the influence of the stars on the lives and fortunes of people: *The horoscopes in Newsday are written by an expert in astrology.*

te pronounced [et].

theist see **agnostic**.

thletics see **-ics**.

at this moment in time see moment.

attorney pronounced [aturney] see power of attorney.

auger/augur: auger a tool for boring holes. augur an official in ancient Rome who foretold the future; more commonly used as a verb meaning to be a sign of the future: *This excellent school report augurs well for your future success.*

au gratin pronounced [oh gratan] a cooking term describing a dish topped with a layer of breadcrumbs and grated cheese, toasted under the grill: *cauliflower au gratin.*

Auntie see BBC.

au pair pronounced [oh **pair**] a foreigner (normally a girl) who does domestic duties for a family who give board and lodging and a small amount of pocket money and treat her as one of them in return.

aural see oral.

authoritative/authoritarian: authoritative describes someone or something with genuine authority or a deep knowledge of a subject: *The engineer assured them in authoritative tones that the dam would not burst.* authoritarian refers to a dictatorial person or style of rule which demands strict obedience: *Victorian fathers were supposed to be authoritarian figures whose children were afraid of them.*

avant garde pronounced [avon **garde**] *noun* people who are daringly modern in their views, especially artists, writers and musicians; *adjective* describes such ideas, people and works: *The council considered the sculpture too avant garde for the shopping precinct.*

avenge/revenge/vengeance all mean to pay someone back for an injury or wrong, but **avenge** is usually to get satisfaction on another person's behalf: *Hamlet should have avenged his father's murder.* **revenge** is usually done on one's own behalf: *He took revenge on his teachers by setting fire to the school.* **vengeance** revenge for oneself or for someone close to one: *The soldier took vengeance on the people who hid terrorists by burning their houses.*

averse see **adverse**.

award/reward: award 1 something such as a prize given to someone, usually in recognition of something well done. *She received an award for bravery for rescuing a child from the river. The theatre had three awards last year.* **2** something given by the decision of a court: *There was an award of £20 000 damages.* **reward** something given as a kind of payment for carrying out certain acts: *There will be a reward for finding the ring. He did not get much reward for all his hard work.*

AWOL absent without leave.

avocado plural **avocados**.

B

B (on pencils) black; **2B** very black.

b born.

BA Bachelor of Arts; British Airways.

B and B, b and b bed and breakfast.

bachelor note the spelling.

backward/backwards as adverbs both are correct, but **backwards** is commoner: *Without looking backwards, he could tell that someone was watching him.* The adjective is always **backward**: *a backward movement. It is a mistake to assume that immigrant children are backward just because their English is poor.*

back-up disk *computers* a disk used for duplicating information already recorded on another disk as a safety measure in case the original is lost or damaged.

bacteria is plural. The singular is **bacterium**: *Streptococcus is the bacterium responsible for sore throats and scarlet fever. Certain bacteria are used in cheese-making.*

bale/bail: to go or **stand bail for someone** to provide money as a security to have someone set free until they are tried etc. **to bail someone out** to have someone set free in this way. **to bail (out)** or **bale (out) a boat** to scoop water out of it to stop it sinking. **to bail out** or **bale out of an aircraft** to leave it by parachute: *When the plane's engine failed, the pilot and all the airmen managed to bale (bail) out over the desert.*

balk/baulk both spellings are acceptable **1** to stop suddenly when confronted by something, especially if it is frightening or repulsive: *In spite of his bold words he balked at drowning the kittens.* **2** to frustrate someone's plans: *Captain Tom balked Henry's plans to stay in London by transferring him abroad.*

banana *adjective* describes a country and also people and things connected with it, especially in Central America, where the economy centres round a single crop such as bananas: *a banana republic.*

bank card/banker's card see **credit card**.

barbaric/barbarian/barbarous all refer to uncivilized behaviour, but: **barbarous** usually refers to the more extreme forms of brutality and unacceptable behaviour: *Barbaric conditions existed in most prisons in the Middle Ages, but the tortures used were utterly barbarous by modern standards.* **barbarian** is used mainly to describe primitive peoples beyond civilization: *The barbarian hordes attacked the Roman city and slaughtered the inhabitants.*

bar see **saloon**.

bar code a pattern of black and white stripes printed on something such as a book, an article in a shop or factory so that it can be identified and checked out when someone scans it with a light pen connected to a computer.

barracks used with a singular or plural verb: housing and buildings for military staff: *The barracks were out of bounds to non-military people. The barracks was a gloomy place in the young officer's eyes.*

barrister/advocate/solicitor: barrister a member of the English Bar, a lawyer who has the right to plead in the higher courts; a member of the Scottish Bar is called an **advocate. solicitor** a lawyer who advises clients, draws up documents, prepares instructions for barristers or advocates, but who represents clients only in the lower courts.

BASIC the most widely used computer language. See **acronym.**

basis the rarely-used plural is **bases**, pronounced [bayseez]: *The bases of their arguments were not valid.*

bath/bathe: bath to wash the whole body in a bathtub: *She usually baths at night.* **bathe 1** to wash or put in water to relieve pain or discomfort: *The miner bathed his sore eyes in cold water.* **2** to swim, to go into water for pleasure: *Bathing in the polluted river caused disease.* **3** in American English = **bath.**

baulk see **balk.**

BBC abbreviation for **British Broadcasting Corporation**; slang **Beeb** or **Auntie.**

BBC English a name used loosely for standard English, describing the pronunciation used by BBC announcers, though nowadays they tend to have more varied accents. See **standard English**.

BC abbreviation for *Before Christ* to indicate the number of years before the birth of Christ: *Julius Caesar came to Britain in 55 BC*. Compare **AD**.

bear see **born**.

beauty/beautiful note the spelling.

Beeb see **BBC**.

beer see **ale**.

beginnings and endings of letters see **letters**.

being often introduces a phrase with an adjective: *being* small; the phrase should be followed by the noun it is describing: *Being small and pretty, she was given the part of the princess by the producer*. This avoids confusion as in: *Being small and pretty, the producer gave her the part of the princess*.

beneath meaning below is now considered rather old-fashioned, except in phrases such as *beneath contempt*. *She married beneath her*.

benefit note the single *t* in the *past* and *-ing* forms: **benefited, benefiting**.

Benelux Belgium, the Netherlands and Luxembourg.

bereaved/bereft both mean having lost someone or something very valuable, but: **bereaved** is usually used to describe a person who has lost someone dear to him or her through death: *The bereaved family were comforted by the tributes to their murdered father.* **bereft** is used in formal language or in literature: *Bereft of his children, his home and his country, he had nothing left in life.*

beside/besides: **beside** means near: *They lived in a cramped cottage beside the canal.* **besides** in addition to: *Don't these children eat anything besides fish and chips?*

between you and me is always correct. See **I/me**.

betwixt meaning between is no longer used except in the phrase *betwixt and between* meaning in the middle.

biannual/biennial: **biannual** twice yearly: *The biannual dog shows are held in June and March each year.* **biennial** 1 every two years: *a biennial exhibition.* 2 of a plant, lasting for two years, maturing in the second.

bias: **biased** and **biassed** are both correct. *The government accused the BBC of being biassed against them in reporting the news.*

bill see **account/bill/invoice**.

Bill/Act of Parliament: **Bill** in the United Kingdom, a piece of legislation in draft form which has to go through three readings successfully in the House of Commons, then on to the House of Lords before it becomes an **Act of Parliament** and part of the law.

billion in Europe a **billion** is a million million, but in the USA it is one thousand million.

binary code a number system which uses only two digits 1 and 0 to represent any number. Inside a computer, each piece of information takes the form of a number in **binary code**.

bit *computers* abbreviation for the binary digits 0 or 1.

bitter see **ale**.

black see **negro**.

black humour describes a type of story, play etc in which tragic events are treated as amusing.

blank cheque see **cheque**.

blond/blonde fair-haired. adjective **blond** masculine: *The blond soldier lay dead.* **blonde** feminine: *Blonde girls often wear blue.* Also used as a noun: *He was dancing with a blonde.*

blueprint 1 a photographic print of technical plans or drawing consisting of white lines on a blue background. 2 the original plan of something: *Our plans are still at the blueprint stage.*

BMA British Medical Association.

b.o. B.O. body odour.

bogey/bogie/bogy 1 usually **bogey** or **bogy**, also **bogey man** an imaginary spirit used to frighten children. 2 usually **bogy** a score in golf, that which a good player should achieve for a hole. 3 usually **bogie** a frame on wheels which allows a railway vehicle to go round curves; a small cart or truck.

bona fide pronounced [bona fydy] means 'in good faith' in Latin and is used: **1** in legal contracts, particularly in insurance where a client must inform the insurance company of any facts which affect the risk, eg previous car accidents or serious illnesses such as heart disease. If the client proves not to have been 'a bona fide purchaser' the contract can be made invalid. **2** to mean genuine: *Only bona fide students can use the library.*

born/borne both spellings are used for the past participle of the verb **bear** meaning to carry, to give birth but note the following:

He has borne his troubles bravely.
She has borne six children.
She was born in London.

bouquet pronounced [**book**ay].

box number see **advertisement**.

BR British Rail.

brackets: round brackets (also called **parentheses**) are used to enclose any additional or explanatory remark to the sentence: *Mix three eggs (fresh if possible) and half a cup of cream.* **square brackets** are used to show that the additional remark or explanation is not made by the writer: *Children respond to kindness [The author obviously does not know my daughter].*

breach/breech: breach 1 a break or gap: *The breach in*

the dam wall caused the flood. **2** the breaking of an agreement or rule: *He was sued for breach of contract.* **breech 1** the buttocks, old-fashioned except in **breech birth, breech delivery** describing a birth when the baby's bottom or feet appear first. **2** the back part of the barrel of a gun.

Britain/Great Britain/British Isles/United Kingdom: Great Britain or, less formally, **Britain** means the political and geographical unit formed by England, Scotland and Wales, along with their surrounding smaller islands, including those of the Channel Islands which belong to Britain. The **United Kingdom** is the above along with **Northern Ireland**. (Its full title is the **United Kingdom of Great Britain and Northern Ireland**.) **The British Isles** is the geographical name for the group of islands which is made up of **Great Britain and Ireland**. See also **Eire**.

Brussels sprouts note the spelling.

BSc Bachelor of Science.

BST British Summer Time: British Standard Time.

Bt Baronet.

bucket shop in informal English **1** an institution which deals or gambles in an unlawful way in stocks and shares. **2** a travel agency which supplies air tickets and holiday packages at cheap prices by using irregular trade practices.

buffet 1 pronounced [bufay] or [boofay] or [boofay] food, usually cold, served where people can serve themselves; a place where food is served in this way; a small restaurant where snacks are served, especially in a railway station. **2** pronounced [**buffit**] to knock about, to strike: *The boat was buffeted by the waves.*

bureau pronounced [**byoo**ro], plural **bureaux** or **bureaus**, both pronounced [**byoo**rose] **1** an office: *the information bureau.* **2** a kind of writing desk.

burn: burnt and **burned** are both used for the past tense but the first is commoner, except when the verb has no object: *The fire burned all night.*

business letter see **letters**.

but sentences can sometimes begin with **but:** *I opened the door and crept in. But what was that terrible shape in the darkness?* Compare **and**.

butch describes: **1** a woman, especially a lesbian, who behaves or dresses in a masculine way. See **homosexual**. **2** a very masculine man.

by-law/bye-law both are acceptable.

byte *computers* a group of eight bits representing a piece of information in a computer. See **bit**.

C

C centigrade; Celsius; Conservative; one hundred.

c cents.

CA Chartered Accountant.

cactus plural **cactuses** or **cacti** pronounced [**cact**eye].

caddie/caddy: caddie a person who carries golf clubs for someone else. Also used as a verb: *He caddied for Jack Nicklaus.* **caddy**, usually **tea caddy**, a box for tea.

caesarean (section or **operation)** note the spelling; pronounced [**sez**airean]: *It was a difficult birth and the baby was born by caesarean section.*

CAL abbreviation for **Computer Assisted Learning** a computer language for writing programs which are used to teach various subjects.

calamine/camomile: calamine a soothing lotion containing zinc oxide used for sunburn and skin irritations. **camomile** a flowering plant, used for example to make a herbal tea.

calendar note the spelling.

calf/heifer: calf male or female young of a cow (also elephant or giraffe etc) under one year old. **heifer** a young cow. The precise meaning varies from region to region.

callous/callus: callous *adjective* 1 cruel, heartless, unfeeling: *Their callous attitude caused him great pain*. 2 of skin, hardened and thickened. **callus** *noun* an area of thick hard skin, especially on the hands or feet.

camomile see **calamine**.

can/may: can formerly meant only to be able to do something, while **may** was used in the sense of to have permission to do it: *I know you can swim, but you may not go into the sea alone*. Nowadays it is acceptable to use **can** in both cases.

cannabis a soft drug derived from the various parts of the hemp plant; if it is smoked or drunk it produces hallucinations. See **hard drugs/soft drugs**.

cannelloni an Italian dish of thick meat-filled pasta tubes. Although plural in Italian, often treated as singular in English: *Their cannelloni is very good*.

cannon/canon: cannon a kind of large gun used in warfare. **canon** 1 a rule, law. 2 a Christian priest connected with a cathedral.

canvas/canvass: canvas *noun* strong coarse cloth used for sails, tents etc. **canvass** *verb* to try to get support from others, eg votes at an election. *The election is tomorrow and he has been out canvassing all week*.

capital letter is used for the first letter:

1 at the beginning of a sentence.

2 of proper nouns: *York*.

3 of important words in titles: *Waterways of Great*

Britain. (See **titles of works**.)

4 of the name of a relative you are addressing: *I am scared, Mummy.*

5 of words connected with religion: *the Koran, Jesus, Judaism.*

It is also used for the pronoun I.

capitalism pronounced [capitalism] a political system or theory which favours private ownership of property, a free market and a minimum of state control. *adjective* **capitalist**.

carat/carrot: carat a measure of the weight of a precious stone or of the proportion of gold in an alloy. **carrot** a root vegetable.

carburettor/carburetter both spellings are acceptable.

carcass/carcase both spellings are acceptable: *Six sheep carcases (carcasses) were delivered to the butcher.*

caries pronounced [caireez] a medical term meaning decay, especially of the teeth: *dental caries.* The adjective is **carious**.

cash card see **credit card**.

caster/castor both spellings can be used for: **1** a small wheel at the base of furniture. **2** a container for sugar, salt etc. **caster** is commoner nowadays. **caster sugar** a finely-ground white sugar.

catalyst 1 *chemistry* a substance that increases the rate of a chemical reaction but does not change permanently itself. **2** a person or thing which, while not changing themselves, bring about changes in other people or things: *The plague acted as a catalyst in bringing about much-needed improvements in living conditions.*

catch 22 a situation in which a person cannot win because one course of action depends on another one, which in turn depends on the first. For example, if he gives a good reason for taking a certain course of action, the very fact of being in a position to act or reason in that way makes nonsense of his case: *The pilot asked to be exempted from suicide missions on the grounds of insanity, but he was refused because it was argued that men had to be insane to take part in them. He was in a catch 22 situation.*

CBI Confederation of British Industry.

CD (in French *Corps Diplomatique*) Diplomatic Corps.

cedilla a mark placed under a letter to show the pronunciation, eg in French under a *c* to show that it is pronounced [s] not [k]: *façade* [**fassahd**].

Celsius see **centigrade**.

Celtic/Gaelic: Celtic pronounced [**keltic**] or [**seltic**] refers to: **1** the **Celts** a people in ancient times. **2** the language of their descendants, containing two groups: **P-Celtic**, consisting of Welsh, Breton or Cornish and **Q-Celtic** consisting of Irish, Scottish and Manx Gaelic. **Gaelic**, pronounced [**gaylic**] or, especially in Scotland [**galic**], one of these languages; the word **Gaelic** alone usually refers to **Scottish Gaelic** and **Irish Gaelic** is often known as **Irish**.

centi- (from Latin; compare **hecto-**) used with other words to mean: **1** a hundredth: *centilitre; centigram.* **2** a hundred: *centipede.*

centigrade/Celsius both refer to the temperature scale which has 100 degrees between the freezing-point and the boiling-point of water: *In Britain temperatures rarely rise above 75 degrees centigrade (Celsius). Compare* **Fahrenheit.**

Central America see **America.**

ceremonial/ceremonious both refer to rituals, dress and activities performed on special occasions: *The gold chain is part of the Mayor's ceremonial dress. Everybody wore full uniform for the ceremonious regimental parade.* However:
   ceremonious also refers to extreme politeness or too much formality: *With a ceremonious bow from the waist, Mr Wixted introduced himself.*
   ceremonial is also used as a noun: *The service was carried out with due ceremonial.*

chagrin pronounced [**shagrin**] a feeling of sorrow and annoyance: *Arabella, dressed to perfection, waited for Henry, but to her chagrin, he asked another woman to dance.*

chamois 1 pronounced [**shamwa**] or [**shamee**] a kind of wild goat found in mountains. **2** also **shammy,** pronounced [**shamee**] (a piece of) soft leather (formerly made from the skin of this goat), often used for polishing.

change adjective **changeable.**

charge account see **credit account**.

charisma [karizma] a special quality (beyond simple attractiveness) possessed by an outstanding person: *In addition to charm he had charisma and thousands followed him.* adjective **charismatic** [karizmatic].

château plural **châteaux** or **châteaus**; pronounced [shatose] a castle or large country house in France.

chauffeur pronounced [showfur] or [showfer].

chauvinist pronounced [showvinist] a person who has a blind belief in the superiority of his own nation, party, sex etc. **male chauvinist pig** name for a man who in a narrow, unthinking way regards women as inferior to men. The adjective is **chauvinistic** pronounced [showvinistic].

cheque a piece of paper issued by a bank or other financial organization by means of which one can pay money to someone else or withdraw money from an account (see **current account** under **account**).
    To fill in a cheque one must add:
the date
the name of the person or organization being paid
the amount of money (in words and in figures)
the signature of the account holder
    Sometimes one is asked to **endorse** a cheque; this means to sign it on the back, sometimes adding one's name and address. See **endorse**.

    blank cheque a signed cheque where no sum of

money is stated and the holder fills in the amount for himself, usually because the sender does not know the exact cost of a purchase or service. As a safeguard the sender can write the instruction 'not to exceed £X', but the practice is best avoided altogether.

crossed cheque a cheque marked in such a way that the chance of fraud is reduced because it can only be paid into a bank account and cannot be exchanged directly for cash. Two parallel lines are drawn diagonally across the cheque and various phrases are written in between them, eg *& Co, account payee only, not negotiable.* Some cheques are already crossed by the bank in printed form, as many people prefer always to use crossed cheques for safety.

open cheque one that has not been crossed (and can therefore be exchanged for cash, eg in a shop).

cheque book journalism a method used by some newspapers to get sensational stories. Large sums of money are paid to criminals, their relatives, friends or victims for the sole right to tell their story.

cheque card see **credit card**.

chip *computers* abbreviation for **microchip** a tiny piece of silicon containing a set of electrical circuits forming part of the whole system of circuits inside a computer.

chiropodist pronounced [shiropodist] or [kiropodist].

chord/cord: chord in music, a number of notes played together. **cord 1** a string: *spinal cord, vocal cord.* **2** fabric, especially corduroy.

chronic see **acute**.

Christian name see **first name**.

CIA Central Intelligence Agency (of the USA).

CID (UK) Criminal Investigation Department.

c.i.f. cost, insurance, freight, a term used in exporting to mean that the price quoted includes transport and insurance to the foreign country. Compare **f.o.b.**

circumflex a mark placed above a letter to show pronunciation, eg in French: *rôle.*

cirrhosis note the spelling: *Cirrhosis of the liver is a serious disease which can be caused by drinking too much alcohol.*

clandestine pronounced [clandestine]: *The banned political party was forced to hold clandestine meetings.*

classic/classical both describe something which is of lasting high quality and in many cases they are interchangeable. However, there are some differences in use: **classic** *adjective* describes: **1** an example of first-rate literature or art or other works: *Freud's classic study on dreams.* **2** something typical of its kind: *a piece of classic stupidity; a classic case of love on the rebound.*

    classical *adjective* describes: **1** music and literature of high quality. **2** the culture, art, literature etc of ancient Greece and Rome. *People visit Athens to tour the ruins of classical temples.*

classified advertisement see **advertisement**.

clause a part of a sentence which has its own subject and verb. The main clause is called the **principal clause** and a less important clause is called a **subordinate clause**: *Nigel punched the boy who had stolen his bicycle pump.* The principal clause is 'Nigel punched the boy' and the subordinate clause is 'who had stolen his bicycle pump'.

clean/cleanse both mean to remove dirt, but **cleanse** also suggests getting rid of impurity or harm: *This oil will cleanse your skin to remove all trace of harmful dust.*

clerihew a nonsensical verse, consisting of four lines of varying length, often about a well-known person:
Henry Irvine
Was utterly unswerving
In his total dedication
To recitation.

cliché pronounced [**kleesh**ay] a word or phrase which was once lively and meaningful but has lost its impact through overuse: *sex rears its ugly head, the proud papa, the blushing bride, a bouncing baby.*

client/clientele pronounced [kleeon**tel**] a **client** is a customer who buys a service rather than goods: *a hairdresser's clients, a lawyer's clients.*

  clientele is a collective noun for clients or

customers: *The Hilton's clientele includes millionaires and film stars.*

climatic/climactic/climacteric: climatic referring to the climate: *The changeable climatic conditions in the British Isles upset people who like constant warmth.*

climactic refers to a climax, a high peak of experience or intensity of feeling: *A climactic beating of the drums signalled the entry of the tribal chief.*

climacteric an important period or event, especially the menopause for a woman, or the corresponding phase in the life of a man.

cm centimetre(s).

CND Campaign for Nuclear Disarmament.

CO Commanding Officer.

c/o care of, at the address of.

COBOL abbreviation for **Common Business-Orientated Language** a computer language for processing business information, files, lists etc.

c.o.d. cash on delivery.

codicil see **will**.

C of E Church of England.

Col. Colonel.

col column.

colander note the spelling; pronounced [**culander**]: *Strain the vegetables in a colander.*

colloquial refers to the language of everyday informal speech which is not appropriate in formal situations, eg *What's up, mate?*

colon 1 introduces a list of items: *The survival pack should contain: waterproof matches, knife, string, glucose and a plastic sheet.* **2** links two clauses where the second in some way develops the first: *Excessive intake of tea and coffee is an addiction: caffeine is a drug.*

Co. company.

Co. Ltd. see **limited company**.

comma 1 separates items on a list: *he was tall, handsome, wise and rich.*

  2 marks a phrase which is an addition to the sentence: *Milly, who is supposed to be my best friend, has spread those tales about me.*

  3 is used after a phrase containing a participle (see **participle**): *Having arrived late, I was given the leftovers to eat.*

  4 is used after the name of someone you are addressing: *Samantha, do stop nagging!*

  5 following words which introduce direct speech: *Nelly yelled, 'Get out and stay out'.*

  6 to separate a phrase or subordinate clause from the main part of the sentence: *On the spot where he died so long ago, his mother still lays a bunch of flowers.* See also **letters**.

commit note the spelling; **committed, committing,** but **commitment:** *They are all committed followers of the*

Women Factory-workers' Party.

committee used with a singular verb if it is necessary to emphasize the unity of the committee members: *The committee of nine unanimously condemns the traitors to death.* If the emphasis is on the committee as a number of separate individuals, a plural verb is used: *The committee are not in agreement about mixed saunas at the leisure centre.*

common noun see **noun**.

communal pronounced [**com**yunal]: *Robert enjoyed communal living and willingly sharing the household jobs and expenses in the commune.*

communism/Communism: communism a political system or theory based on property being held and shared by everyone in a country or community. **Communism** a political movement which aims to put such a system into action. The adjective is **communist** or **Communist**: *They hold communist views. He is a Communist and belongs to the Communist Party.*

compact the noun is pronounced [**com**pact]: *a face powder compact.* The adjective is pronounced [com**pact**]: *a compact little suitcase.*

compact disk a system of making sound recordings on a small disk which does not wear out, by means of lasers; it gives a fine quality of sound with no hissing or crackling.

comparable pronounced [**com**parable]: *The amount of paper produced here is not comparable with the* *amount produced in Sweden.*

comparative adjective see **adjective**.

compare with/to: compare with is used to assess the similarities and differences between two things: *Compare travelling by road with rail travel and you will find each has its advantages.* **compare to** is to say that one thing is like another: *The workers often compared the boss to Hitler.*

compass points see **north**.

complement/compliment: complement 1 a person or thing that completes something: *Red wine is a complement to a fine dish of beef.* **2** the complete amount or number required: *We have not got our full complement on this boat until the fifth crew member returns from shore leave.* **compliment** an expression of praise or admiration: *We all like to receive compliments. I must compliment you on your good taste.*

compound the noun and adjective are both pronounced [**com**pound]. The verb is pronounced [com**pound**] to make something worse by adding a new damaging element: *He broke into the school then compounded his crime by blaming it on his friend.*

comprehensive insurance covers a car owner for damage to another person or property and legal costs, for accidental damage, fire and theft of the insured person's vehicle; it can also cover loss of personal belongings and provide heirs with a sum of money if the insured person dies in the accident. Compare

third party insurance.

comprise/consist of/be composed of all mean to be
made up of many parts: *The course material*
comprises (consists of) a video cassette, a text book
and answers. The household is composed of five
adults, two children and a dog.

Con. see **Conservative.**

concerto plural **concertos** a piece of music for orchestra
along with one or more solo instruments: *a piano*
concerto by Mozart.

conjugal pronounced [**conjugal**]: *Marriage suited*
Ernest and he and Beryl settled down to a life of
conjugal happiness which lasted until their golden
wedding.

conjunction a word used to join two parts of a sentence
together. *And* and *but* are conjunctions which join
two equally-important parts: *They came home and*
then they left again. Others, such as *because*
although, when join an additional part of the
sentence to the main one: *He came because he*
wanted to.

connection/connexion both are correct but connection is commoner.

connoisseur note the spelling; pronounced [coneser*
Being a connoisseur of Italian wine he could spot the
genuine one immediately.

consensus agreement of opinion or evidence. Used with

seek, find, reach: *The chairman refused to ban smoking unless the council reached a consensus.*

consent see **assent.**

conservative/Conservative: conservative being against too much change, especially violent changes. **Conservative** of or supporting the main right-wing political party in Britain, sometimes called the **Tory Party.** It is in favour of property-owning, a free market and a limited amount of state control. Shortened to **Con.** or **C.**

conservatory/conservatoire both words mean a school or institute of music, but **conservatory** also means a greenhouse, especially one attached to a house.

consist of see **comprise.**

contagious/infectious: contagious describes a disease spread by physical contact: *Keep away from other children during the epidemic because measles is contagious.* **infectious** describes a disease transmitted by air or water: *Don't come near us with that cold, Basil, it's infectious.*

continent/Continent: continent one of the great land masses of the earth: *the five continents.* **Continent** mainland Europe as seen from the British Isles: *We're going to the Continent this summer.*

continual/continuous: continual describes things that happen repeatedly but do not go on all the time: *Hippox have had continual losses throughout the football season.* **continuous** describes something that never stops: *There's been continuous rain since lunchtime.*

control past **controlled.**

controversy pronounced [**controversy**] or [contro-**versy**]: *The banning of traffic in the city centre caused such a controversy that people are still arguing as to whether it has helped or hindered the shopkeepers.*

cord see **chord.**

corps pronounced [**kor**] a group of people working together officially: *the diplomatic corps; the Pioneer Corps.*

correspondent/co-respondent: correspondent 1 a person who writes to someone else: *I am a bad correspondent, but I will write at Christmas.* **2** a journalist: *the foreign correspondent of the Times.* **co-respondent** a legal term in divorce cases for the person with whom the husband or wife has committed adultery.

cosmonaut see **astronaut.**

council/counsel: council a group of people who organize, advise or control others; *town council;* its members are **councillors.** Note that members of the Privy Council are called **counsellors. counsel 1** a formal term for advice. **2** the legal name for a barrister (in Scotland an advocate) acting for a person in a law court: *the counsel for the defence.*

counterproductive producing the opposite of the desired effect: *Publicity about the dangers o* *smoking can be counterproductive and even tempt children to start smoking.*

countersign to sign (a document) after someone else has signed it (usually to show that one approves or agrees to it): *Madam, this cheque is made out to your husband, so he has to countersign it before we can put it into your bank account.*

covenant a legally-binding agreement to make regular payments eg to a charity, with the advantage that the organization receiving the money can reclaim tax on the covenanted amounts. **deed of covenant** a document arranging such an agreement.

covering letter see **letters**.

Coy Company.

Cpl Corporal.

credit *in business and commerce* 1 the right-hand side of an account (see **account**) on which payments are recorded. If there is more on that side than on the debit side (see **debit**), the account is said to be **in credit**. 2 to buy something **on credit** means to buy it without paying cash and to pay for it later. See also **credit account** and **credit card** and compare **hire purchase**. 3 the amount of time which a business allows its customers between receiving goods and paying for them. *We can only give you one month's credit.* 4 the amount of money a customer is allowed to have owing — see **credit card** and **credit rating**.

credit account, also called **charge account** an

arrangement with a shop etc whereby one can buy goods without paying cash (often by producing a card and signing the bill); a bill is sent later, usually at the end of each month.

credit card/cheque card/cash card/bank card/ banker's card:

credit card a card which allows one to buy without paying cash at the time (**on credit**); it is provided by a bank or other financial organization which gives each customer a certain amount of credit (say £300) at a time. A bill is sent out, usually each month, for everything one has bought using the card during the previous month. If payment of this bill is late, the customer is charged interest on the payments.

cheque card, also called **bank card** or **banker's card** a card used with a cheque to guarantee that the bank will pay the owner's cheques up to a certain amount. Usually it is necessary nowadays to have such a card in order to pay for something by cheque in a shop etc. The number on the card is copied onto the cheque so that the owner can be traced through the bank.

cash card a card used to withdraw money from a bank account. It can be put into a machine from which one can withdraw money by pressing certain buttons. It can also be used in a bank instead of a cheque.

credit rating a calculation, eg by a credit-card company, of how much credit a customer should be allowed. See **credit** and **credit card**.

crevasse/crevice: crevasse pronounced [crevasse] a

very deep split especially in the ice of a glacier. **crevice** pronounced [**crevice**] a smaller, narrower split, especially in rock or the stones of a building.

criteria is plural. The singular is **criterion**: *Several criteria are used in selecting students for this course: school results, age, previous work experience.*

crochet pronounced [**crosher**] or [**croshay**]. The past tense is **crocheted** pronounced [**crosherd**] or [**croshayd**].

crossed cheque see **cheque**.

CSE abbreviation for Certificate of Secondary Education, an examination taken in Britain (apart from Scotland) at the end of secondary school up to 1987, the highest grade in the examination being equal to a pass in the GCE. See **GCE**.

cu., cub. cubic.

curb/kerb: curb a controlling influence: *The government is introducing new taxes to put a curb on spending. verb* to control tightly: *Curb your tongue!* **kerb** the row of paving stones at the edge of a pavement. (Note that American English has **curb** for all these usages.)

currant/current: currant a dried fruit: *currants and raisins.* **current** *noun* a flow or stream: *The boat was swept downstream by the current. adjective* belonging to the present time: *His current girlfriend is not as pretty as the last one.*

current account see **account**.

curriculum vitae (see also **covering letter** under **letters**) a brief personal history with details of education and work experience usually presented with a job application, often shortened to **cv**. An example might be:

NAME   Simon Dock

ADDRESS   3 Eaves Close, Lamphill
LO6 2BA

DATE OF BIRTH   6 April 1956

MARITAL STATUS   Divorced

EDUCATION
Lamphill High School, 1967-73
A level Art, grade A
A level History, grade B

EMPLOYMENT   1974-1977 Quality Art Mart Ltd, Crossland: trainee assistant valuer, specialising in watercolours.

1977-80 Arty Facts Ltd, Garswold: Sales Manager, specialist in rural pottery. Doubled turnover in first year; initiated links with museum shops in all major cities.

1980-   Hasker Gallery, London: Manager; responsible for buying and selling and exhibitions; 3 assistants; introduced catalogues on video cassettes; 25% sales increase.

INTERESTS   Pottery, painting, antique
swords, sailing.

REFEREES
Mr Solomon Dron, Manager
Arty Facts Ltd, Garswold GN3 6IA

Mrs Leila Hasker, Director
Hasker Gallery
6A Old Bond St, London W1

Note that employers sometimes prefer to have the
applicant's work experience listed with the most recent
first.

cursor *computers* a small sign, often a flashing light,
which marks the place on the screen: *You can move
the cursor by pressing the space bar.*

ynical/sceptical: cynical describes a person who
thinks the worst of others and assumes low motives
behind their actions: *The boss is cynical enough to
take it for granted that his workers fiddle their
expenses.*
  sceptical pronounced [**skep**tical] describes
someone who is not easily convinced of the truth of
certain theories: *She is sceptical about the belief that
soya beans give protection against radiation
poisoning.*

D

d died.

daisy wheel a type of print wheel used with a printer or
typewriter, shaped like a flower with the characters
round the edge and producing good quality print by
striking a character against a ribbon. See **printer**.

dash is used: 1 to separate groups of words in order to
sum up or add to what has already been said: *Bring*
clothes, books, money — everything you need for a
long journey.

  2 instead of brackets: *Jane — fool that she is — has*
lent him £1 000.

  3 when direct speech is left unfinished: *'Well, I'll be*
—', he muttered.

data plural of **datum**: *Make sure your data are correct.*
However, **data** is now widely used and accepted as
singular: *The data on plant life along the motorway*
is fascinating.

database *computers* a large store of information held in
a computer and organized so that the different parts
can be sorted, grouped or extracted easily. In a
business it might contain information about each
customer, including names, addresses and credit
ratings.

date see **letters**.

datum see **data**.

daughter-in-law plural **daughters-in-law**.

debenture a document setting out the terms of a loan. A company needing to raise money for a particular project or fixed period may issue debentures. The holders of these receive a fixed interest annually which is paid out before shareholders receive any interest. An advantage over shares is that the company can buy back debentures.

debit *accounting* a record of money owing which is placed on the left side of an account. When there is no money in the account, only money owing, it is said to be **in debit**. **debit an account** to record a sum of money as a debt in an account.

debut pronounced [**daybyoo**] a first appearance, eg on the stage: *She made her debut at the London Coliseum*.

deca- used with other words to mean ten (times) having ten: *decade* (pronounced [**decade**] a period of ten years). **decathlon** (a contest in which each athlete competes in ten events).

deci- used with other words to mean a tenth: *decimal*.

decision tree (also called a **tree diagram**) a diagram to help a person or organization, especially in a business, to choose the best course of action by setting out various possibilities and showing the likely results.

deed of covenant see **covenant**.

deeds see **title deeds**.

de facto pronounced [dayfacto] or [deefacto] in fact, i practice, rather than by law or rule: *The rebels threw th president into prison and became themselves the d facto government.* Compare **de jure**.

default *computers* anything which a computer does a a matter of course unless instructed to do otherwise *The default colour for lettering on his computer scree is white.*

defective/deficient: defective means faulty: *A defectiv pipe allowed gas to escape causing four death* **deficient** means lacking an important element: *Som slimming diets are deficient in essential vitamins.*

definite/definitive: definite clear, without any doub *The general gave a definite order to retreat, but the misunderstood it.* **definitive** refers to something whic cannot be altered or improved on: *Look up Kin Percival's reign in Smith's definitive work on th subject.*

definite article the word *the*. Compare **indefini article.

de jure pronounced [dayjury] or [deejury] by righ according to law: *the de jure government.* Compar **de facto**.

delivery note see **advice note**.

delusion see **allusion**.

Democrat/Democrat: democrat a person who supports democracy. **Democrat** a member or supporter of the Democratic party, one of the two main political parties of the USA. Compare **Republican**.

Dep., Dept. department: deputy.

ep. depart(s).

dependant/dependent: *noun* **dependant,** occasionally spelt **dependent,** a person who depends on another for support: *She has three dependants — two children and her mother.* The adjective is always **dependent:** *She has two dependent children.*

deposit account see **account.**

deprecate/depreciate: deprecate to express disapproval of, to make to seem unimportant: *Grandfather tended to deprecate his children's efforts instead of encouraging them.* **depreciate** to go down in value: *Luxury cars depreciate rapidly after a few years.*

de rigueur pronounced [dereeger] necessary according to certain rules, eg of fashion *Hats will be de rigueur at their wedding.*

derisive/derisory both mean mocking, scornful: *'You are not very bright, are you?'* she said with a derisive (derisory) laugh. However, **derisory** also means deserving scorn or mockery, ridiculous: *Ten pounds is a derisory sum to offer for a gold watch.*

desiccate note the spelling: to dry, especially food in order to preserve it: *desiccated coconut.*

desk-top publishing the production of high-qualit
printed material with layouts suitable for new
sheets, leaflets, booklets etc by using a persona
computer and printer. This avoids the need to sen
the material to a professional printer.

despatch see **dispatch**.

develop note the spelling: **developed, developing**.

devolution an increased degree of self-governmen
granted to a region of a country: *Some Welsh peopl*
believe that devolution would solve many of Wales
problems.

diaerisis [diairisis] two dots over a vowel to show that i
is to be pronounced separately from the vowel befor
or after it: *Noël* pronounced (noel]. Compare **umlau**

dialect see **accent**.

diaphragm note the spelling.

diarrhoea or **diarrhea** note the spelling.

different from/to: different from is considered mor
correct: *Chinese medicine is different from Europea*
in some respects. However, **different to** is widely use

dingy/dinghy: dingy drab, dirty: *The poor lived in da*
dingy huts. **dinghy** a small boat: *They went ashore i*
the dinghy.

Dip. Diploma.

Dip. Ed. Diploma in Education.

diphthong two vowels pronounced as one and sometimes written or printed as one letter: *æ* in *mediæval* is a diphthong. The tendency now is to replace the diphthong with the letter which represents the sound: *medieval*.

direct pronounced [di**rect**] or [die**rect**].

disc/disk an object with a round flat shape: *a gramophone disc;* formerly the **disk** spelling was used mainly in American English, but it is now widely used also in British English for the storage device in a computer; this can be either a **floppy disk**, made of thin plastic or a **hard disk** of inflexible material, on which computer programs and data can be recorded by means of a **disk drive**.

disciple see **apostle**.

discreet/discrete: discreet tactful, careful about what one says: *The bank clerk passed Ted a discreet note about his overdraft.* **discrete** in formal English, separate.

disinform to give people false information usually for political purposes: *The government disinformed people about the sinking of warships to hide the bad news.*

disinterested/uninterested: disinterested impartial: *The mother of the accused was hardly a disinterested onlooker in the dispute.* **uninterested** not interested: *Eileen's infatuation with Tom made her quite uninterested in other boys.*

disk see **disc**.

disk drive a device attached to a computer which allows storage of software on a floppy disk. See **disc**.

disorientated/disoriented both are acceptable: *After spinning round in the dance, Hetty was too disorientated (disoriented) to find her partner for a moment.*

dispatch/despatch both spellings are acceptable, but the first is now commoner: *The packages were dispatched (despatched) in time for the early train.*

distinct/distinctive: distinct 1 clearly different: *There are seven distinct colours in the rainbow.* **2** clear, noticeable: *There is a distinct taste of coffee in these biscuits.* **distinctive** different because of some special feature: *Everyone recognizes the south coast of England because of the distinctive white cliffs.*

distrust/mistrust both mean to treat someone or something with suspicion, but: **distrust** means to regard someone or something as definitely wrong or dishonest and **mistrust** means to have strong doubts without proof.

ditto see **do**.

dividend a share of the net profits of a company paid to a shareholder or a share of the profits of a cooperative society paid to its members.
    pay dividends to bring an extra advantage or bonus: *All his hard work will pay dividends if he passes the exam.*

division lobby see lobby.

DIY do-it-yourself.

DJ disc-jockey.

DLitt Doctor of Letters.

DM Deutsche Mark(s).

do. short for ditto meaning the same thing, and sometimes used eg in a list to avoid repeating the same name etc:

> London Borough of Brent
> do.   do. do. Ealing

Often double commas are used instead:

> London Borough of Brent
> „   „   „ Ealing

don/fellow: don a senior member of a university college particularly at Oxford or Cambridge. fellow 1 an established or regular member of a university college, especially Oxford or Cambridge. 2 a researcher at a university who is paid for a limited period to do a piece of research.

dot-matrix printer a type of printer used with a computer or a typewriter. The head is a set of fine pins which hit the ribbon in the shape of the required character.

double negative see negative.

doubtful/dubious: doubtful 1 having doubts: *The airmen were doubtful about the safety of the helicopters after three accidents.* 2 causing doubt uncertain: *You can't depend on warm weather in June because British weather is always doubtful*

dubious 1 causing doubt, often in a bad sense: *I won say Edmund swindles people, but his busines. activities are often dubious.* 2 having doubts: *Many people are dubious about the value of nuclea weapons.*

dove/hawk: **dove** a politician who favours peacefu ways of coming to terms with a possible enemy. **hawk** a politician who prefers aggressive methods: *Th doves in Congress persuaded the hawks to sue fo peace.*

down payment see **hire purchase.**

downward/downwards either is correct as an adverb *Leaping from the cliff he hurtled downward(s).* As a adjective only **downward** is correct: *It was easier t walk on the downward path.*

draft/draught: **draft** 1 a rough outline, a sketch: *Mak a rough draft of your essay, then write it neatly.* 2 a order to a bank for the payment of a sum of money 3 in American English, the ordering of people by th government to join the armed services; a group c people so joined: *He escaped the draft by emigratin* **draught** 1 a current of air. 2 an amount of liqui drunk. 3 the amount of water a boat needs to float *Narrow boats with a shallow draught are used o canals.* 4 beer drawn from a barrel. In America English, all these meanings are spelt **draft.**

ream the past is **dreamt** or **dreamed**.

rier/dryer both spellings are acceptable.

rugs see **hard drugs/soft drugs**.

Sc Doctor of Science.

SO Distinguished Service Order.

ubious see **doubtful**.

ue to/owing to: due to should follow a noun: *The crash was due to carelessness.* It is commonly used as a preposition: *Due to a childhood illness, he had a limp.* However, many consider this unacceptable. **owing to** is accepted as a preposition: *Owing to a childhood illness, he had a limp.*

warf plural **dwarfs** or **dwarves**.

ing/dyeing: dying is part of the verb to **die**: *All the flowers are dying.* **dyeing** is part of the verb to **dye**: *The teenagers are all dyeing their hair red this year.*

E

each when **each** comes before the word it refers to it is followed by a singular verb: *Each of the victims (each victim) has an unusual scar.* When it comes after the word it refers to it has a plural verb: *The victims each have an unusual scar.* **each other/one another** both are correct and can be used in the same way: *The people in our street always try to help each other (one another).*

east see **north**.

economic/economical: economic refers to the economy or financial state, especially of a country: *The discovery of oil has improved the economic conditions of several Middle Eastern states.* **economical** describes something or someone not wasteful: *Small cars are usually the most economical on petrol.*

ECU European currency unit.

ed editor; edited by; edition.

edible/eatable: edible fit for eating, suitable as food, not poisonous or harmful: *Are you sure these mushrooms are edible?* **eatable** worth eating, good to eat: *The apples were so shrivelled they were not really eatable.*

EEC European Economic Community.

effect to cause or bring something about: *The manager effected an increase in production by introducing modern machinery into the workshop.* See also **affect**.

efficacious/effective/effectual/efficient: efficacious especially of a medicine, producing the desired result: *A substance derived from foxgloves is an efficacious treatment for heart disease.*

effective 1 having the desired result: *Double glazing is an effective method of keeping the house warm.* **2** actual, real: *The new law is effective from today. He is the effective ruler of the state; the president is just a figurehead.*

effectual capable of producing the desired result (not necessarily completely effective): *Heavy sentences should be effectual in the fight against drunk driving, but the police have no clear picture as yet.*

efficient able to perform duties or functions well: *An efficient washing machine is a great help in the home. An efficient manager.*

EFL/ESL/ESP All refer to English taught to people who do not speak it as a native language. **EFL** (English as a foreign language) refers to English taught to foreign students not normally resident in the UK. **ESL** (English as a second language) refers to English taught to immigrants and to other people who use English in addition to their own language. **ESP** (English for special purposes) refers to English taught to foreigners who need it for their professions.

EFTA European Free Trade Association.

eg/ie: eg for example (from Latin *exempli gratia*): *Let us discuss a famous writer, eg Shakespeare.*

   ie that is to say (from Latin *id est*) is used to define more clearly what has gone before: *The child is suffering from epidemic parotitis, ie mumps.*

EGM extraordinary general meeting.

ego 1 a psychological term for the conscious mind or personality of an individual. **2** a person's self-image: *Your compliment should boost Tom's ego.*

egoist/egotist: egoist a person who bases his or her philosophy on self-interest: *James admitted that he was an egoist, but argued that by looking after himself first he was only doing what most people do anyway.*

   egotist a person who is self-centred, not from conviction, like the egoist, but from selfishness: *The talented child of adoring parents, he became a complete egotist with no regard for the needs of others.*

Eire/Ireland/Irish Republic/Northern Ireland: Eire (pronounced [aira]) and **Irish Republic** are names for the part of the island which is independent of Britain. **Ireland** can be either **1** the geographical name for the whole island, including Northern Ireland. **2** another way of referring to Eire or the Irish Republic. **Northern Ireland** the part of Ireland which belongs to

Britain as part of the United Kingdom. See also
Britain.

either pronounced [eyether] or [eether] can be used to
link two singular words that are the subject of one
verb; the verb must be singular: *Either the dog or the
cat has stolen the Sunday joint.* If one of the subjects
is plural, the verb must also be plural: *Either Prince
Andrew or his brothers fly helicopters.*

elder/eldest, older/oldest: both are used as comparatives of **old**, but **elder/eldest** are usually used in
descriptions of ages within a family: *Zak is my elder
brother and our eldest brother is Joel aged thirty. Joel
is older than Zak.*

electric/electrical/electronic: electric describes
something powered by electricity: *an electric organ,
an electric iron.*

 electrical refers to something which may be more
generally connected with electricity: *electrical
engineering, electrical goods.*

 electronic refers to complex electrical devices using
transistors and valves: *Our office uses modern
electronic equipment.*

embarrass note the spelling.

emend see **amend**.

emigrant/emigré/immigrant: emigrant a person who
has left his native country to settle in another. *verb*
emigrate; the verb is commoner than the noun.

 emigré a person, often French, Russian or Polish,
who has fled his country for religious or political

reasons: *The Polish emigrés had a club in London.*

immigrant a person coming into a country to settle there: *Immigrants find the British climate difficult to get used to.*

eminent/imminent/immanent: eminent well-known, distinguished, excellent of its kind: *The club was addressed by an eminent surgeon.*

imminent about to happen (very soon): *The beating of the native drums meant that an enemy attack was imminent.*

immanent a formal or literary word meaning found within or throughout something: *the immanent peace of the landscape. God is immanent in the universe.*

encyclopaedia/encyclopedia both spellings are acceptable.

endemic see **epidemic**.

ending a letter see **letters**.

endorse 1 to sign the back of a document, usually a cheque or money order etc: *Granny endorsed the page in her pension book so that we could collect her money from the post office.* See also **cheque**. **2** to write official comments on a document: *Alan has had his driving licence endorsed twice for speeding offences.* **3** to approve or support a claim or statement: *The foreman put in a claim for overtime pay and the works manager endorsed it.*

endowment assurance a type of life insurance which

provides a tax-free sum of money for the insured person at the end of an agreed number of years, or for his heirs if he dies earlier.

enquire/inquire both are correct and the meaning is the same, but note: *a Court of Inquiry. We are making further inquiries.*

ENT Ear, Nose and Throat.

entomology see **etymology**.

entrée pronounced [ontray] a French word found on menus, referring either to a main course in a meal or to a course between the main courses.

envelope both [**en**velope] and [**on**velope] are acceptable pronunciations, but [**on**velope] is rather old-fashioned. *verb* **envelop** pronounced [en**vel**op] to wrap, surround or cover: *The hut was enveloped in flames.*

envy/jealousy both refer to a very strong desire for something which another person possesses but:
    envy is simply an overwhelming wish to have what the other person has: *She watched with envy as the neighbours got into their new car.*
    jealousy contains a strong element of resentment that somebody has got what you feel you deserve more than they do: *Grandma's favouritism towards his twin aroused fierce jealousy in Mark.*

epi- used with other words to mean on, above; after; in addition to: **epicentre** (the area above an earthquake); **epidural** (on or outside the dura mater, the outer covering of the spinal chord): *Epidural injections can be given to remove the pain during childbirth.*

epidemic/endemic used of diseases but also (figuratively and informally) of other conditions:

epidemic (an outbreak) affecting large numbers of people in a particular place at a particular time: *There was an epidemic of cholera here in 1956. Measles has reached epidemic proportions with a third of the village children affected. Reduction in the police force has resulted in an epidemic of crime.*

endemic affecting people in a particular area usually over a long period of time: *Where there is a poor water supply, certain diseases are endemic.*

equities ordinary shares. See **stocks and shares**.

ER Queen Elizabeth (in Latin *Elizabeth Regina*).

escalate to move upwards in measurable stages rather than just to increase: *The war escalated to the extent that the number of frontline troops doubled every two months.*

ESL see **EFL**.

ESP extra-sensory perception; see also **EFL**.

especially/specially: especially, also in very informal English **specially** particularly: *Pale-skinned people are especially sensitive to bright sunlight.* **specially** for a particular purpose: *He had the house specially built to accommodate his family of fifteen.*

Esq. (abbreviation for **Esquire**) a rather old-fashioned and very formal word for Mr; it follows the name and is used in addressing a letter: *Darren Pym, Esq.*

est. established.

esthetic see **aesthetic**.

etc abbreviation for **etcetera** (meaning and other things in Latin); pronounced [etsetra]: *Bring your unwanted junk to the jumble sale including books, cast-off clothes etc.*

ethnic 1 refers to the division of humans into different races: *The education committee tries to provide teachers for ethnic minorities in the city, including pupils of Asian and African origin.* **2** describes loosely any arts, crafts, music etc of races with different traditions from native British ones: *Tessa is very eccentric. She goes in for ethnic rugs and oriental religions.*

etymology/entomology: etymology the study of the origins of words.

   entomology the study of insects.

euphemism pronounced [**yoo**femism] a milder, pleasanter, more amusing word to replace the usual term for an unpleasant, tragic, or embarrassing thing: *to pass away* = to die; *the cloakroom* = the toilet; *merry* = drunk.

even can change the meaning according to where it is placed in the sentence:

   1 *Even David can understand Physics.* (Here 'even' refers to David. Physics is so simple; so much so that an ignorant boy can understand it.)

2 *David can even understand Physics.* (Here 'even' refers to understand. David is so clever that in addition to his other talents he can understand Physics.)

3 *David can understand even Physics.* (Here 'even' refers to Physics. He can understand many things and also, surprisingly, Physics.)

every one/everyone: **every one** means each individual person or thing: *I looked at all my sweaters and every one had a hole in the elbow.* **everyone** means all people considered as a group and is followed by a singular verb: *Everyone shops at the supermarket in our town.*

exaggerate note the spelling: *'Thousands of people came to my party,' Celia exaggerated, trying to impress Ethel.*

exceptional/exceptionable: **exceptional** out of the ordinary: *It is exceptional for a baby to start walking at the age of eight months.* **exceptionable** giving cause for criticism or complaint: *I find his habit of arriving uninvited at all hours most exceptionable.*

excess a term used in motor insurance whereby the insured person agrees to pay a proportion of the cost of any claim he makes: *The insurance company only refunded £250 of the £300 repair bill because I had agreed to pay £50 excess.*

exclamation mark used in place of a full stop at the end of a phrase or sentence to indicate strong emotion:

Look out, it's behind you! It can appear in brackets immediately after a word which is expected to surprise the reader: *War is wonderful (!) but so time-consuming.*

executor see will.

ex gratia (Latin); pronounced [ex**gray**sha] of a payment, made by special decision and not because it has to be made: *The company has no obligation to rehouse flood victims, but the management are making ex gratia payments of £5 000 to every family as a gesture of goodwill.*

exhaustive/exhausting both mean tiring, but: **exhausting** is the usual word for this meaning: *Working in the heat is exhausting.* **exhaustive** means thorough, leaving nothing out: *The Police made exhaustive enquiries, interviewing every person in the village about the incident.*

ex officio (Latin); pronounced [ex o**fish**eeoh] holding an appointment automatically because of some other position: *The Chairman of the company is an ex-officio member of the Planning Committee.*

expert system *computers* a type of computer program containing a large amount of specialized information, such as legal or medical data. The user can type in a query and receive answers on topics which normally require consultation with an expert.

expletive a violent exclamation to relieve the feelings, such as: *Drat! There's no milk left!*

exquisite pronounced [exquisite] or [exquisite]: *The Georgian desk is exquisite with its rare carvings and elegant shape.*

extra- used with other words to mean outside, beyond the limits of something: *extraterrestrial; extra-special.*

F

F Fahrenheit.

faeces/feces pronounced [**feeseez**] a formal or medical word for waste matter from the body, the contents of the bowels; the second spelling is commoner in American English.

Fahrenheit a temperature scale in which the freezing point of water is 32 degrees and the boiling point 212 degrees. Compare **centigrade**.

faithfully: Yours faithfully see **letters**.

family name/surname/second name all mean the name by which all the members of a family are known as distinct from their individual first names.

second name is also used for an additional name added to the first name; it may be an individual or a family name: Jane *Alice* Bryan; William *Curtis* Brown.

family name may also be used for a first or second name which is traditional or popular within a family: *My father and two of my cousins are called Bramwell because it's an old family name.*

Some people use a double or 'double-barrelled' surname: *William Baring-Gould; Robert Penn Warren.* If the name has a hyphen it will be found under the first word, eg in a telephone book. If there is no hyphen, it will appear under the last word. Thus *Baring-Gould* will be under B, while *Penn Warren* will be under W.

See also **first name**.

farther/further comparatives of **far**. Both are correct when referring to distance: *We could not walk further* (or *farther*) *than thirty miles a day.* Only **further** can be used with reference to time and extent: *The night clubs were closed until further notice. No further information about the dead men will be released until their families have been told of the accident.*

fascinated followed by **with** or **by**: *Children are fascinated with* (or *by*) *stories about dinosaurs.*

father-in-law plural **fathers-in-law.**

fawn/faun: fawn 1 *noun* a young deer. **2** *noun, adjective* (of) a light brownish colour. **3** *verb* to try to get someone's favour by flattery: *The courtiers fawned on the Emperor and encouraged him to think he was a god.* **faun** a Roman god, half man, half goat.

FBI Federal Bureau of Investigation (of the USA).

fearful/fearsome: fearful 1 a rather formal word meaning afraid, frightened or causing fear: *Fearful of the dark streets, she took a taxi.* **2** used informally to mean very bad, awful: *What a fearful mess.* **fearsome** causing fear, fierce: *a fearsome beast.*

feces see **faeces.**

feet see **foot.**

fellow see **don.**

female/feminine/feminist: female of the female sex: *female bird. The female has brown feathers.* **feminine** describes qualities normally associated with women rather than men: *The flowing lines of the dress are very feminine.* **feminist** describes attitudes supporting the rights of women.

fetus see **foetus**.

fewer/less: **fewer** is used to refer to numbers of individual things or people and is followed by a plural noun: *Nowadays fewer women are full-time housewives.* Less refers to an amount or mass: *Less milk is drunk in France than in Britain.*

f and the following lines, page *etc.*

fiancé/fiancée pronounced [feeonsay] both mean a person who is engaged to be married but: **fiancé** is a man and **fiancée** is a woman.

fictional/fictitious: **fictional** describes a character existing only in fiction: *Count Dracula is a fictional character based on a historical tyrant called Vlad.* **fictitious** untrue, not genuine: *To avoid arrest, he gave a fictitious address to the police.*

fiddle an informal word for a violin; also used informally to mean cheating: *They're on the fiddle again. He fiddled the books for two years before he was caught out.*

fig. figure; figurative.

figurative refers to words and expressions such as a simile or a metaphor when they are not being used literally: *The butter mountain is a figurative expression which brings to our notice just how much surplus butter Europe produces.*

finale/final: finale pronounced [feenahly] **1** the las part of a performance in a theatre etc. **2** the last part o a musical work. **final** describes something which happens at the end: *Oliver's final word wa 'goodbye'.* Also used as a noun to mean the last (an most important): *the cup final. She sits her finals i June.*

finalize to complete negotiations or plans, especiall in business. Nowadays it often means simply t complete, although not everybody approves of th second usage.

financial/fiscal both refer to money matters, but **financial** refers to the management of money i general and **fiscal** refers to government finance an taxation in particular: *The senate altered the fisc laws to raise money for the war.*

first/firstly both can be used to mean to begin with *First* (or *firstly*) write your name on the paper, the answer three questions.

first name/Christian name/given name/forename a mean the personal, individual name as distinct fror the surname of a person. However, **given name** an **forename** are used in formal and written languag **first name** is a useful term in a society which include many non-Christians. See **family name**.

first person the grammatical forms of pronouns an verbs when they refer to the speaker. *I, me, we, u* are first person pronouns. See also **second person** an **third person**.

fiscal see **financial**.

fjord/fiord pronounced [fyawd] or [feeawd] a narrow arm of the sea, especially in Norway. Both spellings are acceptable.

flaccid pronounced [flasid] or [flaksid] a formal word meaning soft, limp, not stiff: *The flower stems lay flaccid on the ground.*

flammable/inflammable both mean able to burn, but there is a dangerous and widespread assumption that **inflammable** means not likely to burn. Manufacturers tend now to label goods **flammable** and **non-flammable**.

flaunt/flout: flaunt to make something very obvious in a conceited way: *She wore furs and flaunted her jewels in front of her poor cousin.* **flout** to go against something in an obvious way, thus showing one's contempt: *By leaving early she was flouting the rules.*

flautist/flutist both words mean a person who plays the flute, but **flautist** is commoner in British English and **flutist** in American.

flier/flyer both spellings are acceptable.

floor in Britain, the floor at ground level is called the **ground floor** and the next level up is the **first floor** and so on; in America, the **first floor** is the one at ground level and the next level up is the **second floor** and so on.

floppy disk see **disc**.

flotsam/jetsam: 1 outcasts from society, the poor and homeless: *The Salvation Army help the flotsam and jetsam of modern society.* **2** useless old rubbish. As legal terms, a distinction is made between **flotsam** goods found floating on the sea, and **jetsam** goods which have been thrown overboard from a ship and washed ashore.

flounder/founder: flounder to move (about) with difficulty, eg in mud or snow; to be unable to act or do things successfully: *Harry is obviously floundering because he has no experience of finance.* **founder 1** of a ship, to fill with water and sink. **2** to collapse, fail: *When the sales fell so low, his business foundered.*

flout see **flaunt**.

flutist see **flautist**.

flyer see **flier**.

f.o.b. free on board, a term used in exporting to mean that the price quoted includes the cost of carriage insurance etc until the goods are on board the ship or aeroplane. Compare **c.i.f.**

focus the past can be either **focused** or **focussed**: *He pointed the camera at the crowds, then focussed on the happy face of one little girl.*

foetus/fetus both spellings are acceptable: *Many people who are against abortion consider that the foetus is already a human being whose life is important.*

folk plural **folk** or **folks**: **folk** is used when referring to people in general: *The Archers is a radio serial about country folk*. **folk** is used informally to refer to a person's family: *Bob lives away from home, but he sees his folks at weekends.*

foot/feet: foot the usual plural is **feet**, but with numbers **foot** is also commonly used: *The giant was nine foot seven inches tall.*

for-/fore-: used with other words: **for-** originally meant not or against: *forbid, forsake*. **fore-** means in front or beforehand: *forerunner, foretell*. Occasionally confusions arise: the *foreword* of a book/ *forward* the adverb to *forbear*/a *forebear* (also spelt forbear) an ancestor.

forceful/forcible: forceful strong, powerful, having effect: *forceful arguments; a forceful personality*. **forcible** using force, either physically or by putting pressure on someone's mind: *The police had to make a forcible entry by smashing the front door open. He produced such forcible arguments against dog licences that nearly everyone voted to abolish them.*

forename see **first name**.

formal refers to speech, behaviour etc which follows the rules very strictly, rather than following everyday usage and habits: *The headmistress was very formal in her dress and in speech and insisted on the girls wearing gloves and calling her Madam*. Compare **informal**.

formal letters see **letters**.

format 1 the general appearance and layout of a published work: *Teenagers like the lively format of the new magazine which give plenty of space to pictures of pop stars.* **2** the general appearance or order of a show, a plan etc. **3** *computers* the layout or display on a screen. Also used as a verb (past **formatted**) to prepare a disk for use in a computer. *We formatted five disks.*

former/latter: former refers to the first of two persons or things mentioned, **latter** to the second: *There were two applicants for the job, Smith and Eccles, the former being the director's nephew and the latter his son.* To refer back to items in a longer list, use **first, second** etc and **last.**

formidable pronounced [**for**midable]: *A giant of a woman with a deep voice, Mrs Blenkinsop struck terror into her pupils with her formidable presence.*

formula plural: in technical usage **formulae**, in less formal use **formulas.**

forte pronounced [**for**tay] a person's strong point: *Although Mick draws well, it is clear from his exhibition that painting is his forte.*

Fortran a computer language used mainly for writing scientific and mathematical programs.

fortunate/fortuitous: fortunate lucky: *How fortunate you were to inherit a million pounds.* **fortuitous** accidental: *His success in business is quite fortuitous owing nothing to his skill but to the fact that all his competitors died in the earthquake.*

forward/forwards both are correct when an advancing movement is intended: *Grandma leaned forward (forwards) to poke the fire.* Otherwise only **forward** is correct: *We put the clock forward in summer.* The adjective is always **forward**: *a forward movement.*

founder see **flounder**.

foyer pronounced [foyay] or [fwayay] or [foyer] an entrance hall in a theatre, hotel etc: *Milly sells ice cream in the foyer of the Palace Theatre.*

FP former pupil.

Fr franc(s).

fracas pronounced [fracka] a noisy quarrel: *After the fracas in the café, the waitress swept up the broken glass.*

freehold/leasehold both are ways of having legal rights over land and property, but: **freehold** means absolute rights without any time limits. **leasehold** means that the leaseholder has the use of the land or property for a limited period only and usually pays a regular fee or rent for it.

friendly letters see **letters**.

ft. foot, feet.

fuchsia note the spelling: pronounced [fyoosha]: *The brilliant red of the fuchsia in flower lent colour to the patio.*

-ful note the spelling of words ending thus: *spoonful*, plural *spoonfuls; cupful*, plural *cupfuls*.

fulfil past **fulfilled**; note the spelling: *Little Benny never fulfilled his early promise after his first concert, because his voice broke.*

fullness/fulness both are acceptable: *The slimming biscuits work by giving people a feeling of fullness after eating them.*

full stop marks the end of a sentence; also called a **period**. See also **abbreviations**.

fully-blocked business letter see **letters**.

furore pronounced [fewrory] or [fewraw] 1 a public outcry against something: *The release of the murderer caused a furore.* 2 an outburst of public enthusiasm for something: *There was a furore in London when the new short skirts came into the shops.*

further see **farther**.

further education/adult education both describe education given after the normal school-leaving age (apart from the courses in universities or other degree-granting institutions) but: **further education** is given in colleges which offer courses in both vocational and non-vocational subjects. **adult education**, while not excluding vocational and examination courses, takes place in colleges where the emphasis is on leisure and recreational subjects.

G

g gram(me)(s).

Gaelic see **Celtic**.

gambit 1 in chess, an opening move in which a risk is taken to gain a later advantage. **2** any opening comment or move: *His gambit was to ask so many questions that there was no time to start work.*

gamble/gambol: gamble to play a game of chance, to bet on the result of a game or sport: *Patrick gambled all his money away at the races.* **gambol** to skip and jump about in a playful way: *The children were gambolling about in the spring sunshine.*

gaol/jail both are correct: **gaol** is used in official terminology; only **jail** is used in Scotland and America.

garage pronounced [garazh] or [garidge] in British English; [garazh] in American English.

gas plural **gases**.

gay 1 jolly, merry. **2** homosexual.

gazump to raise the price of a house after previously agreeing verbally to a lower figure. The reason is usually because another buyer has offered a higher price: *The very day we had arranged to buy* *the cottage we were gazumped by a wealthy businessman.*

GB Great Britain.

gbh grievous bodily harm.

GCE abbreviation for **General Certificate of Education** a public examination at the end of pupils' secondary education in the United Kingdom (until the late 1980s) apart from Scotland which has the **Scottish Certificate of Education (SCE)**. See also **A-level** and **O-level**.

GCSE abbreviation for **General Certificate of Secondary Education** which, as from 1988, is the public examination to be taken at the end of secondary school in place of the GCE and CSE. See **CSE**.

Gen. General.

-generation a word which combines with numerals such as first, second etc to mean belonging to a certain stage of development in manufacture and often used to describe computers or weapons: *First-generation computers in the forties were so bulky they occupied large rooms.*

ginger group a small active group within a larger group or society whose aim is to stimulate the others into livelier action: *The young mothers formed a ginger group to urge all the women to fight against the closing of the hospital.* Compare **pressure group**.

gipsy/gypsy both spellings are acceptable.

given name see **first name**.

gm gram(me)(s).

GMT Greenwich Mean Time.

gourmand/gourmet both mean a person who loves good food but: **gourmand** one who eats too much; **gourmet** pronounced [goo-may] one who appreciates good food and wine and knows a lot about them.

govt. government.

GP general practitioner.

gram/gramme both spellings are acceptable.

grammar the rules for the combination of words into sentences and for the use of various forms of words: *English grammar is considered easy because nouns and verbs do not change their endings much.*

gramophone note the spelling.

grand-/great- both prefixes can combine with uncle, aunt, niece, nephew but nowadays **great-** is more common: Thus the uncle of one's parent is one's *great-uncle* (or *grand-uncle*).

graffiti followed by a plural verb: *The graffiti on bridges are difficult to erase.*

graphics a picture or diagram drawn by a computer and displayed on a screen or printed out by a plotter or printer. It can be used with a singular or plural verb. See also **plotter** and **printer**.

grave a mark placed above a vowel to show pronunciation, eg in French: *à la carte.*

gray/grey both spellings are acceptable.

great- see **grand-**.

Great Britain see **Britain**.

Grecian/Greek both describe things and people connected with Greece, but: **Grecian** is used to refer to works of art, literature and classical Greek culture: *The museum has an exhibition of Grecian urns.*

grey see **gray**.

grisly/grizzly/gristly: **grisly** causing a feeling of horror: *The newspapers were full of the grisly details of the murder in the cowshed.*

    grizzly *adjective*, also **grizzled** of a greyish colour: *His hair is still dark but his beard is grizzly. noun,* also **grizzly bear** a kind of large greyish-brown bear.

    gristly full of gristle: *a gristly piece of meat.*

ground floor see **floor**.

guarantee note the spelling.

guerrilla/guerilla both spellings are acceptable, but the first is commoner: *The peasants were skilled in guerrilla warfare because they knew the mountains well.*

gung ho a slang expression for misplaced and exaggerated enthusiasm: *We were appalled at the minister's gung ho attitude to a war which might have terrible consequences.* Compare **jingoism**.

gunwale/gunnel both pronounced [**gunn**el] the upper edge of the side of boat.

guru 1 a Hindu or Sikh religious leader. 2 any leader or

a religious group or cult who guides the spiritual
progress of the others: *His guru recommended
meditation and special exercises.*

uttural note the spelling: *His guttural accent made
Alice think he might be German or Dutch.*

ynaecology/gynecology both spellings are acceptable; pronounced [gyneecology].

ypsy see **gipsy**.

H

H note that the name of this letter is aitch [aytch]
H (on pencils) hard; **2H** very hard.

hackneyed describes a word or phrase used so ofte
that it has lost its original force: *His speech to t*
school leavers was full of hackneyed references to 't
big world outside'.

had/have note the following: *if he had seen it; if Ma*
had known. In phrases such as these *if he had ha*
seen and *if Mary had have known* are not acceptabl

haemo- see **hemo-**.

haemorrhage see **hemorrhage**.

hallo/hello/hullo are all acceptable greetings.

handful plural **handfuls**. See **-ful**.

handwritten letters see **letters**.

hang the past is normally **hung**: *The cage u*
hung from the ceiling. With reference to capi
punishment, murder or suicide, the past is **hange**
Children were hanged for petty crimes.

hangar/hanger: **hangar** a large building for housi
aircraft. **hanger** a support on which things can
hung.

harakiri form of suicide practised in Japan in which the belly is slashed with a dagger, originally because the person was in disgrace.

harass pronounced [harass]; note the spelling: *Mrs Turner was so harassed that she left one of the children behind in the park by mistake.*

hard copy see **printout**.

hard drugs/soft drugs: hard drugs are those extremely dangerous and addictive drugs such as heroin, cocaine and LSD.

soft drugs are those such as marijuana and cannabis which are illegal and not advisable, but less addictive than hard drugs.

hard porn/soft porn: hard porn means the type of pornographic film, book, picture or play which is considered obscene according to the law, usually portaying sexual acts and perversions which might corrupt people.

soft porn means the type of publication, film or play etc which deals with sex less openly and offensively and is not illegal: *Some newspapers try to attract readers with soft porn such as pictures of nude girls.*

hardware/software *computing* **hardware** includes all the pieces of equipment used in computing such as the computer itself, the monitor etc.

software means all the programs which tell the computer what to do. These include programs built into the computer when it is made, as well as the programs which the user gives to it: *Software games* *for your computer can be bought on a cassette or a disk.*

hardwood/softwood: hardwood the wood of broadleaved trees which lose their leaves, eg oak, beech, teak, mahogany, used for high-quality furniture.

  softwood the wood of evergreen conifers such as pine, used for general building purposes.

have: must of is occasionally written in mistake for **must have** and is not acceptable. It occurs through confusion with **must've**: *I must've left my glasses at home.* See also **had**.

hawk see **dove**.

HB (on pencils) hard black.

headings see **letters**.

hecto- (from Greek; compare **centi-**) used with other words to mean a hundred: *hectogram*.

heifer see **calf**.

hello see **hallo**.

hemi- (from Greek; compare **semi-**) used with other words to mean half: *hemisphere; hemiplegic* (paralysed on one side of the body).

hemo- or **haemo-** used with other words to mean blood: *hemoglobin; haemophiliac*.

hemorrhage/haemorrhage both spellings are correct but **hemorrhage** is commoner.

hetero- used with other words to mean other, different: *heterogeneous* (of different kinds, varied); *heterosexual* (sexually attracted to people of the opposite sex).

hiccup/hiccough: both are pronounced [**hiccup**].

Hindi/Hindu: Hindu a follower of the Hindu religion usually a native of India. **Hindi** one of the languages of India.

hire/let/rent: hire and **rent** can mean 1 to have temporary use of something in return for payment: *It costs a lot to rent (hire) a car on holiday.* 2 to allow a client or customer the temporary use of something in exchange for payment: *British Waterways rent (hire) canal boats to tourists.*

   let has only the second meaning: *Mr Grundy lets flats to temporary workers in town.*

hire purchase a system of buying in which one pays by instalments, ie a certain amount is paid each week or month etc until the total has been paid, including the interest which is charged for this method of paying. Often a larger sum has to be paid at the time of purchase and this is known as a **down payment**.

historic/historical see (a/an for use with indefinite article) **historic** describes events or people important in history: *the historic landing on the moon.* **historical** refers to history or events from history: *The story of Robin Hood is a mixture of historical fact with fiction.*

HIV virus see **AIDS**.

HMS Her/His Majesty's Ship (used for warships).

HMSO Her/His Majesty's Stationery Office.

HNC Higher National Certificate.

HND Higher National Diploma.

hoard/horde: **hoard** a large amount or store of something: *They kept a hoard of ammunition in the loft.* **horde** a very large crowd of people (originally nomads or fighting men): *The Mongolian horde swept over the plains. Hordes of football supporters swarmed through the gates.*

hoi polloi pronounced [hoypoloy] (from Greek) the common people, often used contemptuously: *Not wanting to mix with the hoi polloi, Clarissa dined in her room.*

holding company a company set up to hold a controlling interest in the shares of one or more companies.

holocaust massive destruction and loss of life. It is used particularly to refer to the murder of millions of Jews by the Nazis during the Second World War.

homely 1 like home, comfortable: *I like the homely atmosphere in this modest little restaurant.* 2 plain, not good-looking: *Without make-up Samantha's face looks quite homely.*

homeopathy/homoeopathy both spellings are correct but **homeopathy** is commoner; an unconventional way of treating illnesses by the use of drugs which are capable of producing symptoms that are similar to those of the disease being treated.

homosexual/lesbian: homosexual (a person who is) sexually attracted to people of the same sex; this word can refer to men or women: *She is a homosexual. They have a homosexual relationship.* **lesbian** of a woman, (one who is) sexually attracted to other women: *The Monday play on Radio 4 is about a lesbian schoolmistress.*

honorary describes: **1** a title, position etc held by someone who has not done the normal work or fulfilled the usual requirements for it, but who was awarded it as an honour: *The Prince was awarded an honorary degree by Manchester University.* **2** an unpaid position: *Lady Flavia is the honorary president of the Girls' Guild.* It is often abbreviated to **Hon**: *Hon. Secretary: E J Brown.*

hoof: hoofs/hooves both are possible plurals.

hopefully 1 in a hopeful way: *to travel hopefully.* **2** it is to be hoped: *Hopefully I will pass my exam.* This is a fairly new usage, but there is no reason to condemn it.

horde see **hoard.**

hors d'oeuvre pronounced [orderv]: *Nelly served shrimp cocktail as an hors d'oeuvre while the roast was cooking.*

hospice 1 in former times, a shelter for travellers, especially one kept by monks or nuns. **2** nowadays, a special hospital for very ill or dying people.

hospitable two pronunciations are acceptable [**hospitable**] and [**hospitable**].

HP hire-purchase; also **hp** horsepower.

HQ headquarters.

hr hour.

HRH Her/His Royal Highness.

hullo see **hallo**.

human/humane: human to do with mankind: *the human race*. **humane** kind, merciful: *The zoo treated the animals in a humane way.*

hung see **hang**.

hung parliament refers to a situation in which no political party has a big enough majority to rule effectively and therefore the party in government has to depend on cooperation from another party when voting takes place on important issues.

hygiene/hygienic note the spelling: *Liza was so keen on kitchen hygiene that she soaked the cloths in bleach every night to kill the germs.*

hype modern slang abbreviations of hyperbole, meaning excessive enthusiasm for, or promotion of something which does not deserve it: *Media hype turned an ordinary courtship into a fairytale romance.*

hyper- used with other words to mean above, more than normal: *hypercritical.*

hyphen is used to show both separation and joining of words and syllables:

1 It separate words into two parts if part of the word comes at the end of a line and the other part at the beginning of the next line:

There was a beauti-
ful young princess.

2 It shows disjointed speech: *'P-pp-please go, B-bob', he stammered.*

3 It joins two or three words together to form one word: *multi-racial; sister-in-law.* It is hard to give strict guidelines on when to use hyphens, especially as there is a growing tendency to avoid them; for example, when the word becomes very common, the hyphen is often dropped: *The council has multiracial policies.* But note the following:

(1) The pronunciation or meaning of some words is made clearer by the use of a hyphen: *co-author; de-icer.*

(2) Some pairs of words are distinguished by the use of a hyphen: *recover* to get better / *re-cover* to cover again.

(3) Some prefixes are usually followed by a hyphen: *ex-army; non-intervention.*

(4) When two or more words are used as an adjective before a noun, a hyphen can sometimes avoid confusion: *a fine-tooth comb.*

(5) Nouns and adjectives made up of verb + preposition or adverb usually have a hyphen (unless they are written as one word): *take-off; make-up.*

(6) Compound numbers between *twenty-one* and *ninety-nine* are usually hyphenated.

hypo- used with other words to mean below, under, less than normal; *hypodermic* (under the skin); *hypothermia* (a condition where the body temperature is abnormally low, often suffered by elderly people in very cold weather).

Hz hertz.

I

I/me I is the subject pronoun, **me** is the object: *He and I decided to break off the engagement at the same time. Mother said she blamed neither him nor me. This information is between you and me.* However, note the following: *Who's there? It's me.* In informal English, **It's me** is so widely used that it has become more acceptable than **It is I.**

-ible see **-able**.

-ics nouns ending in *-ics* sometimes have a singular verb and sometimes a plural. When the noun refers to a science, an academic subject, sporting activity etc, it has a singular verb: *Athletics is Bernard's strong point at school but Mathematics is his next best subject. Acoustics is a branch of physics. Statistics is now widely taught.* Otherwise it has plural verb: *The acoustics of the hall are excellent. These statistics are not reliable.* See **acoustics**.

idiom 1 a group of words which has a particular meaning that may be quite different from the usual meaning of the words used separately: *The foreign visitor who did not understand the idiom 'jail-bird' thought we were discussing our parrot's cage.* 2 language that is natural to a speaker: *The nasal tones and witty Liverpool phrases were the idiom of* *the Beatles.* **3** a particular artistic style and use of materials: *Finely-carved ivory with delicate lines was Bernard's idiom.*

ie see **eg.**

if ... were/if ... was in an imaginary or supposed situation:

   if ... were is more acceptable in formal English: *If Stanley were more attentive to his wife, she would be less irritable.*

   if he/she/it was is tolerated in informal English: *If she was my daughter I'd send her to boarding school.* But:

   if I were ... is considered more correct: *If I were you I'd take an aspirin.*

illegible/unreadable: illegible especially of hand writing, not able to be read: *Your scrawl is quite illegible.* **unreadable** refers to something not worth reading because it is boring, confused, complicated etc. *Paul's memoirs are unreadable because he was already losing his mind when he started on them.*

illusion see **allusion.**

immanent see **eminent.**

immigrant see **emigrant.**

imminent see **eminent.**

immoral/amoral: immoral wrong according to an accepted moral code: *It would have been immoral for Paul to have a divorce because his religion forbade it*

amoral not accepting or recognizing any moral code: *It's no use appealing to the hijacker's sense of decency when his actions show that he is completely amoral.*

imply/infer: imply to hint or suggest without actually stating something: *The member for Little Hogdown implied that the Prime Minister was a liar but dared not put it into so many words.* **infer** to deduce from the evidence that something is true: *As Tom was staggering and his speech was slurred we had to infer that he was drunk.*

in inch(es).

Inc. Incorporated.

incl. including.

incredible/incredulous: incredible unbelievable, amazing: *It is incredible that the boy who fell into the bear pit escaped unharmed.* **incredulous** unwilling to believe: *People were incredulous when Angus claimed to have seen the Loch Ness monster.*

indefinite article the word *a* or *an*. See **a/an** and compare **definite article**.

indenting see **paragraph**.

independent note the spelling.

index plural **indexes** or **indices**; the second is mainly used in mathematics.

index-linked of an investment or payment, means that a sum of money has its value protected against inflation. Interest paid on index-linked investments keeps pace with a regularly up-dated price list of everyday necessities. Examples are: index-linked pensions, National Savings Certificates and insurances.

indictment pronounced [inditement] an accusation of a crime: *They brought out an indictment against him.*

indoor/indoors: indoor is an adjective describing something inside a building: *an indoor swimming pool.* **indoors** is an adverb meaning into, or taking place in, a building: *When the storm broke we ran indoors.*

infectious see **contagious**.

infer see **imply**.

inflammable see **flammable**.

inflation a financial situation where prices and wages are rising, but production of goods and services is not increasing enough to pay for them.

inflict see **afflict**.

informal refers to speech, behaviour etc belonging to casual, everyday usage: *Martin would stroll along the corridors in informal clothes, never wearing a tie and greeting everyone with a cheery 'Hi there'.* Compare **formal**.

ingenious/ingenuous: ingenious outstandingly clever and skilful: *The ingenious inventor of cats' eyes made the roads much safer for drivers at night.*

ingenuous too trusting and innocent: *It was ingenuous of Sally to believe the man's hard-luck story without checking the facts.*

input *computers* the aspect of computing concerned with putting data and information into the computer.

inquire see **enquire**.

Inst. Institute.

install note the spelling: *He was installed as Chancellor of the University. noun* **installation**.

instalment see **hire purchase**.

insurance/assurance: insurance a way of providing financial protection for property, life, health etc against certain misfortunes such as loss, fire, damage and death. In return for the protection, the insured person pays to the insurers a regular sum of money, called a premium. (See **premium**.) **assurance** insurance which is concerned with events which are certain like death as distinct from possible ones like fire or loss of goods.

integral pronounced [integral] describes an essential part of something else: *Diet alone is not enough because exercise is an integral part of our slimming course.*

intense/intensive both mean done or felt with great force, effort or deep emotion, but intensive is used to describe activities or situations where the efforts are concentrated on one aspect: *While hunting the killer, the police made an intensive search of the area.*

inter- used with other words to mean between, among: *interchange; international.*

interface 1 an electrical circuit linking one device with another especially in computers. **2** any point of contact bringing two different subjects or areas of interest together. This new use of the word is often disapproved of without good reason: *Hong Kong can be seen as the interface between Communist China and the West.*

into/in to: into a preposition meaning: **1** from outside to inside: *Get into bed this minute!* **2** from one state to another: *The ice melted into water.* **in to** is used of a movement inside in order to do something: *Come in to see your cousin.*

intra- used with other words to mean within, inside: *intravenous* (within a vein).

introductions when introducing two people, say *'Mrs Jones, this is Mr White'* or simply *'Mrs Jones — Mr White'* or, less formally, *'Edna, I'd like you to meet my cousin Charles'.* The standard reply when someone introduces a person is *'How do you do?'* The person introduced is also expected to reply *'How do you do?'* Less formal replies are still not approved of by many people; these include *'Pleased to meet you'* or *'Hello'* or simply a handshake.

inv. invoice; invented.

invaluable/valuable both mean worth a great deal, but **invaluable** describes something or someone so highly prized that their value cannot be measured: *A reliable water supply was invaluable to early settlers.*

inventory pronounced [**invent**ry] a detailed list of goods, possessions etc: *Before letting your house, make an inventory of the furniture and fittings in each room.*

inverted commas see **quotation marks**.

invitations formal invitations are usually addressed in the third person and a formal reply should follow the same style.
a formal invitation:

Alan Daniels

Chartered Accountants

*The Partners and Staff of
Alan Daniels*

*request the pleasure of your company
at a Christmas Reception at the
Brine Leas office*

*on Thursday, 18th December 1989
at 4.30 p.m.*

Bartle House Road
Brine Leas
Cheshire BL4 1BS
Tel: 061-083 6471   *RSVP*

Note that RSVP is an abbreviation for French répondez s'il vous plaît, meaning please reply.

A formal reply to the above:

Dr and Mrs David Charles thank the Partners and Staff of Alan Daniels and accept with pleasure their invitation for 18th December 1989 at 4.30 p.m. in the Brine Leas office.

However, most people nowadays prefer to reply with an informal letter to all but the most formal invitations.

invoice see **account**.

inward/inwards either is correct as an adverb: *The boat moved inward (inwards) toward the quay.* As an adjective only **inward** is used: *The outward journey to New York was pleasant but the inward flight to London was long and uncomfortable.*

IOU short for 'I owe you', a piece of paper given to someone from whom you are borrowing money, as a promise that you will return it.

IQ Intelligence Quotient, a measure of intelligence.

IRA Irish Republican Army.

Ireland see **Britain** and **Eire**.

Irish (Gaelic) see **Celtic**.

Irish Republic see **Eire**.

irony/sarcasm: irony a rather mild way of making fun of or criticizing someone by saying the opposite of what is intended: *'Clever boy, Chris, you've burnt the toast as usual,'* she murmured with affectionate irony.

   sarcasm a more wounding type of criticism or mockery using a variety of means, including irony: *'Have you quite finished boring everyone with your stupid stories?'* she asked in a tone of withering sarcasm.

-ise see **-ize.**

italics see **titles of works etc.**

its/it's: its belonging to it: *My car is not in its usual place.* it's the abbreviated form of it is: *'It's a goal!' shouted the fans.*

ITV Independent Television.

-ize/-ise these verb endings, meaning to treat or act in a certain way, are both acceptable; -ise is commoner in British English, but -ize is recommended by the Oxford English Dictionaries: *recognize; nationalize.* There are however a few verbs which are always spelt with -ise; these include: *advertise; advise, comprise; despise; devise; revise; supervise; surmise; suprise; televise.*

J

J joule(s).

jail see **gaol**.

jargon 1 specialized language used for a particular subject or activity: *Computer jargon is creeping into the speech of people outside the profession.* **2** unnecessarily complicated language: *He tried to impress us with his incomprehensible technical jargon.*

jealousy see **envy**.

jetsam see **flotsam**.

jewellery/jewelry both spellings are correct.

jingoism exaggerated patriotism which is expressed in a noisy aggressive way: *The newspaper accused party leaders of jingoism, objecting particularly to the use of marching songs to stir up a hatred of foreigners.* Compare **gung-ho**.

job applications see **curriculum vitae** and **letters**.

joystick *computers* a lever device used with a computer which can be moved in any direction to command the cursor on the screen. It is used especially for computer games.

JP Justice of the Peace; see **judge/magistrate**.

Jr Junior.

judge/magistrate both try legal cases in court but:
magistrate in England and Wales, a minor public
officer who may be a Justice of the Peace (JP) (an
unpaid magistrate who deals with less serious cases)
or a salaried magistrate who has two main functions:
1 to hear and try cases of a less serious nature; **2** to
conduct preliminary inquiries into more serious
offences.

   judge a senior judicial officer who hears and tries
serious offences.

judicial/judicious: judicial refers to judgments or
judges in a court of law: *judicial enquiry, judicial
authority.* **judicious** wise, making good decisions:
*The judicious use of old and new materials made the
housing estate pleasant to live in.*

judgement/judgment both spellings are correct.

K

K: 1 also **Kbyte** *computers* abbreviations for **kilobyte**, the measurement used for the size of a computer's memory: One kilobyte (usually written 1K or 1Kbyte) is enough space for about a hundred words. **2** in informal English and job advertisements **K** is used to mean £1 000: *Salary 12K per annum.*

k kilo.

kerb see **curb**.

keyword *computers* a word in a computer programming language which sets off a chain of reactions inside a computer: *PRINT* and *INPUT* are keywords in BASIC.

kg kilogram(me)(s).

KGB the secret police of the Soviet Union.

kilo kilogram(me).

kilometre [kilometre] and [kilometre] both pronunciations are acceptable: a measure of length in the metric system, equivalent to 5/8 of a mile.

King's English see **Queen's English**.

km kilometre.

kneel the past is **knelt** or **kneeled**.

knit past is **knit** or **knitted**. **knitted** is preferred for the activity of making things in wool or other yarn: *His mother knitted him a woolly vest.* **knit** is preferable otherwise: *It was months before the damaged bones of his arm knit together.*

knock-for-knock agreement an agreement between two insurance companies that when two vehicles with comprehensive insurance (see **comprehensive insurance**) have been in collision, each insurance company pays for the damage to their own client's vehicle, no matter who was at fault.

knowledgeable note the spelling.

KO, ko to knock out.

kph kilometres per hour.

Kt Knight.

kW, kw kilowatt(s).

kWh, kwh kilowatt-hour(s).

L

L Liberal.

LA Los Angeles.

Labour Party the main left-wing political party in Britain, sometimes called **Socialist**, generally in favour of nationalization, trade unions and generous state aid in welfare and social services. Sometimes shortened to **Lab**.

latter see **former**.

lay/lie: lay (past **laid**, past participle **laid**) to put something down: *Lay your wreaths on the coffin now.* **2** to set the table ready for a meal.
 lie (past **lay**, past participle **lain**) to be in a flat position: *Lie down if you're tired. The letters lay on the mat all day.*
Note that the past of **lay** is **laid** and the past of **lie** is **lay**

lbw leg before wicket.

leasehold see **freehold**.

leeward/windward: leeward the nautical pronunciation is [**looard**] but many people also say [**leeward**]; means in the lee or shelter of the wind: *The leeward side of the island was sheltered from the harsh north east wind.* **windward** exposed to the wind: *The windward side of the fortress wa.*

crumbling and weatherbeaten.

eft-wing *politics* describes the views of people who aim at big changes and new progressive policies.

end/loan both mean to allow another person the temporary use of one's property, but **loan** is less common and more formal. *Lend me your pen. The government loaned £5 million to the enterprise.*

esbian see **homosexual**.

ess see **fewer**.

et see **hire**.

etters this section includes:
  notes on different types of letters, with examples:
    typed or wordprocessor letters
    handwritten letters
    formal and business letters (fully-blocked and semi-blocked)
    friendly and informal letters
  information on some aspects of setting out letters, including
    date
    headings
    reference numbers
    signatures
    opening and closing remarks
    beginnings and endings for particular types of letter
  titles and forms of address for people with special titles, and information on how to address them in speech.

Note that the rules for producing clear and acceptabl
letters vary according to the type of correspondenc
and whether the letter is handwritten or typed.

formal letters are those written to people outsid
the family or circle of friends, usually on business, an
can also be called **business letters**. If produced on
wordprocessor or typewriter, they may be:

1 fully-blocked (ie paragraphs are not set in fro
the margin: see **paragraph**) with open punctuatio
or:

2 semi-blocked with open punctuation (ie indente
or inset paragraphs and full punctuation in the mai
body of the letter only).

fully-blocked business letter:

Tel 007 3773   High Trees
                                Lichpole
                                WALWICH
                                Herts HO5 7WC
                                25 March 1987

Your Ref: LT/LB

Mrs Laura Tey
Take-a-Cake Ltd
Unit 2
Garley Industrial Estate
GARLEY
Herts HO2 9RT

Dear Mrs Tey

Thank you for your letter of 3 March 1987.
During the season we require regular weekly
deliveries of cakes, biscuits and breakfast
cereals. I should like to know if you could
supply us with these?

One of our brochures is enclosed for your
information.

Yours sincerely

Tracy Santley

---

semi-blocked business letter with open punctuation. This is an example of a **covering letter** for a job application to go with a completed application form or cv (see **curriculum vitae**):

---

5 Top St
OCKLES
Cheshire
CWO 9AB
7 May 1987

The Principal
Baxter College
SHEMPTON
Essex
EX1 3TU

Dear Sir

    I should like to apply for the post of laboratory assistant as advertised in the Daily Telegraph on Monday 4 May 1987.

    I enclose a curriculum vitae for your information.

        Yours faithfully

        Mary Doss

---

handwritten letters lack the clarity of those produced by machine. For layout and punctuation of a handwritten letter, see example on p. 131.

Some more examples of formal letters.
asking for a reference:

2 Bargate Rd
Byley
BY4 WEC
9 May 1987

Dr T Cammell
Sidney Health Centre
Countess Avenue
Byley
BY2 WOU

Dear Dr Cammell

I am applying for a post as a receptionist at the Chinkley Hospital and wonder if I could give your name as a referee?

As you will remember, I stopped work at your centre in 1981 just before the birth of my first child. Now that my youngest is at nursery school, I feel able to take a part-time job. The post at Chinkley interests me particularly because it requires the sort of experience in dealing with elderly patients which I gained while working at your day centre.

I enclose a copy of the details of the post.

Yours sincerely

Mona Pringle (Mrs)

letter to a local councillor:

2 Bargate Rd
Byley
BY4 WEC
10 May 1987

Councillor Michael Ray
The View
Lower Byley
BY2 WOU

Dear Councillor Ray

As council member for this ward you will
be aware of the plan to hold motor cycle
rallies regularly on Winter Hill. I hope
you will join the residents of the village
in objecting•to this scheme which will
disrupt the peace and pollute the
environment.

I would like to invite you to a meeting
on the subject at Byley Hall on Monday
4 June.

Yours sincerely

Michael Pringle

letter to an insurance company:

> 2 Bargate
> Byley
> BY4 WEC
> 1 June 1987
>
> Emblem Insurance
> High St
> Berkley
> BK1 LEA
>
> Dear Sirs
>
> Policy number 9/1100934
>
> I have to report that I was involved in an accident this morning. Both my car and the lorry I was in collision with are damaged.
>
> The lorry driver is: Ben Allison of 34 Exeter Rd, Cambridge and his insurers are Hexley Insurance Co Ltd, Margaret Rd, Ely.
>
> Yours faithfully
>
> Mona Pringle (Mrs)

letter to a bank:

2 Bargate
Byley
BY4 6EC
2 August 1987

The Manager
Southern Bank
6 Main St
Byley
BY2 40C

Dear Sir

Account number 46758 9800

I enclose a cheque for £800 drawn on the account of Miss P. Oates. I would be grateful if you would credit it to my account.

Yours faithfully

Melita Pringle (Miss)

letters to the press are addressed to the editor and sent to the editorial address printed in the newspaper (not usually the same as the address for advertisements). An example of a letter to a newspaper:

> Rural Delivery
> Howards Line
> Wellington
> New Zealand
> 3 October 1988

The Editor
Wyche Weekly
4 High St
Cheshire
CW2 WRA

Dear Sir

My wife and I would be very grateful for the help of any of your older readers who remember the Dabb family of the Old Crown Hotel. Simon Dabb is my only relative in Britain and it is many years since I last had any contact with him. Perhaps if you publish my request, it will jog the memories of some of the regular customers at the Crown.

I must add my appreciation of your excellent newspaper which is passed on to me by Nelly King of Wellington whose family emigrated from Wyche in 1947.

Yours faithfully

Hartley G Freer

letter of resignation:

1 Yates Parl
Bancorn
Merseyside
MN8 BEI
9 April 1988

K Trant Manager
Hickle and Smith Ltd
8 High Street
Porry
PO7 8CV

Dear Mr Trant

I would like to resign from my post a
assistant archivist in the Records Dept a
from 9 May 1988. My husband has recentl
been posted to West Germany for two year
and I expect to be joining him within the nex
few months.

My six years with the firm have been ver
pleasant and I feel I have gained a lot of usefu
experience. I shall take away happ
memories of the people and the friendl
atmosphere.

Yours sincerely

Sarah Lyons (Mrs)

friendly and informal letters the way to write to close friends and members of the family is a matter of choice, but there are friendly letters to colleagues, people who have given hospitality and acquaintances which need more care. Some examples are:

handwritten letter of thanks for hospitality:

> 33 Filey Gardens
> Warleypitts
> Sussex SW4 8OE
> 6 April 1988
>
> Dear Bernard and Katy,
>
> Thank you very much for your hospitality last weekend. I enjoyed every minute even if it did rain all Saturday.
>
> One of the nicest things about staying with you is always the food. The special Easter lunch was delicious.
>
> With love,
> Carol

letter of condolence on the death of a colleague:

6 Broad Street
Tenterden
Kent CT6 0HQ
4 July 1988

Dear Mrs. Cutler,

We were all shocked to hear of George's death. Everybody in the office had been aware of the seriousness of his illness. His humour and kindness will be very much missed.

If there is anything we can do to help you at this difficult time please let us know.

With deepest sympathy,
Yours sincerely,
Jane Howard

beginnings and endings letters to certain people need particular methods. The most common are as follows:

business letters have the name and address of the person the letter is addressed to on the left side above Dear Sir etc:

The Director
The Museum of Farming
Redley
RY6 7TK

If you do not know the name of the person:
begin   Dear Sir or Madam
end   Yours faithfully

Note that 'Yours truly' can be used instead of 'Yours faithfully', but it is less common nowadays.

If you know the name of the person:
Mr R Joffy, Director
The Museum of Farming
Redley
RY6 7TK
begin   Dear Mr Joffy
end   Yours sincerely

If you know only the name of the organization either:
1 Put any suitable title at the head of the address on the left above Dear Sir or Dear Madam.
Some possible titles are: The Manager, The Manageress, The Personnel Manager: The Secretary,

The Director.

An example of a job advertisement where this is needed might be:

Assistant required for Beauty Department. For further information and application form write to Lovely Lady Enterprises, Clay Lane, Tapworth.

begin   The Manageress
         Lovely Lady Enterprises
         Clay Lane
         Tapworth
         Dear Madam
end   Yours faithfully

or another possibility is:

         The Personnel Officer
         Lovely Lady Enterprises
         Clay Lane
         Tapworth
begin   Dear Sir or Madam
end   Yours faithfully

or :   Lovely Lady Enterprises
         Clay Lane
         Tapworth
begin   Dear Sirs
end   Yours faithfully

However, it is preferable to use the first method when possible, as the other two are very impersonal.

Note that if a woman's name does not show whether she is married or not, **Ms** can be used instead of Miss or Mrs:

Ms Mira Sinclair.

friendly letters:
begin   Dear Alice
end   With love, With best wishes etc

For a more detached relationship:
begin   Dear Alice
end   Yours, Yours ever.

date there are various ways to write the date:
20 April 1989
20th April 1988
April 20 1988
April 20th 1988
20.4.88

headings it is useful to place a brief heading stating the subject of a business letter, including any account numbers, reference numbers which are appropriate:
Dear Sir
   Nancy Grimes: roll number 89898
   Mortgage application

opening remarks simple language is best:
Following our telephone conversation about my daughter's health, I would like to confirm that she ...

With regard to my previous letter of application for the post of assistant matron, I would like to add that ...

Thank you for your letter of April 6 1987 in which you say that ...

reference numbers when replying to a business letter, quote the reference number from their letter

on the left side of your letter either above Dear Sir and
before their address or between Dear Sir and the
beginning of the letter:

Ref: TP/MN

Tranton Brothers
Mankley
MK9 5BT

Dear Sirs

or: Dear Sirs
   Ref 897865 (Loans)

The second method is useful when the reference
number is long.

signatures either first name and surname or initial
and surname are used to sign business letters. If the
name or initials do not make the sex and status clear
it is best to add in brackets after the signature Mr, Mrs,
Miss, Dr etc. Because signatures are not always
legible it is best to write the name in capitals or to type
it below the actual signature:

Yours sincerely

M. D. Pringle

M D PRINGLE (MISS)

closing remarks avoid pompous language. Some
possibilities are:

I should be grateful for your comments on this matter.

I should be grateful for any help/information you can give me.

I would appreciate a reply as soon as possible.

I appreciate all the help which you have given us in this matter.

See also **advertisements, postcard, curriculum vitae** and **invitations**.

   titles and forms of address There are special ways of addressing people with titles in conversation and in letters and the following are some examples, the letters may end either Yours faithfully or Yours sincerely, depending on how formal the contents are:

doctors (medical and others)
in conversation Dr Keefe
in a letter   Dr T Keefe
begin   Dear Dr Keefe

However note that surgeons are addressed and referred to as Mr Brown etc.

clergymen
Protestant churches
in conversation Mr Turner
in a letter
address   The Reverend Ian Turner *or*
                 The Reverend I Turner
begin   Dear Mr Turner

Roman Catholic priest

in conversation Fr Selby, Father
in a letter
address   Fr George Selby *or*
    Fr G Selby
begin   Dear Fr Selby

Rabbi
in conversation Rabbi Jackson, Rabbi
in a letter
address   The Reverend Reuben Jackson *or*
    The Reverend R Jackson
begin   Dear Rabbi Jackson *or*
    Dear Rabbi

armed forces
in conversation Major Beales
in a letter
address   Major D Beales
begin   Dear Major Beales

The Prime Minister
in conversation Prime Minister
in a letter
address   The Right Hon. Athol Jones PC
    MP Prime Minister
begin   Dear Mr/Mrs Prime Minister *or*
    Dear Mr/Mrs Jones *or*
    Dear Prime Minister (informal)

Member of Parliament
in conversation Miss Chantler
in a letter

address	Miss Anita Chantler, MP
begin	Dear Madam *or* Dear Miss Chantler

members of the peerage
in conversation Lord Delamere
in a letter

address	The Earl of Delamere
begin	Dear Lord Delamere

son or daughter of a peer
in conversation Lord Basil, Lady Dora
in a letter

address	Lady Dora Delamere
begin	Dear Lady Dora

knight or baronet
in conversation Sir Horace
in a letter

address	Sir Horace Mole
begin	Dear Sir Horace

dame
in conversation Dame Gertrude
in a letter

address	Dame Gertrude Gurney
begin	Dear Dame Gertrude

woman life peer or wife of knight or baronet
in conversation Lady Mole
in a letter

address	Lady Mole
begin	Dear Lady Mole

Note that the Queen and the Duke of Edinburgh are
treated in a special way as follows:

The Queen
in conversation Ma'am
in a letter   write to her secretary

It is usual for everyone, apart from close friends, to
address communications to:
The Private Secretary to Her Majesty The Queen
Buckingham Palace
London SW1
begin   Dear Sir
end   Yours faithfully

Introduce the subject of the letter by asking that 'Her
Majesty's attention be directed to ...' and refer to the
Queen as Her Majesty the first time, then as The
Queen throughout the letter.

The Duke of Edinburgh
in conversation Sir
in a letter
address   To His Royal Highness The Duke
            of Edinburgh
begin   Your Royal Highness *or* Sir
end   I have the honour to be, Your
            Royal Highness' most obedient
            servant

letters of administration see **probate**.

liable to see **apt to**.

liberal/Liberal: liberal having views which favour
freedom and relaxing of rules: *They have a very*

liberal outlook towards the behaviour of the young.
Liberal of or supporting the **Liberal Party**, one of the major political parties in Britain (sometimes shortened to **Lib.** or **L.**); allied with the **Social Democratic Party** to form the SDP and Liberal Alliance, known as the **Alliance Party**.

libel see **slander**.

licence/license: licence *noun: driving licence.* **license** *verb: Some supermarkets are licensed to sell alcohol.*

lie see **lay**.

lieutenant pronounced [leftenant] or, in North American English [lootenant]. Sometimes shortened to **Lieut**.

life insurance provides a sum of money on the death of an insured person for his heirs. Premiums can be paid throughout the lifetime of the insured person or up to the age of sixty-five. See **premium**.

light pen *computers* a pen-like device connected to a computer to enable the user to draw directly on the computer screen.

like/as/as if: like is used with a noun or pronoun in comparisons: *She looks like a witch and eats like a bird.*

  as is used when actions are compared: *After we are married I shall work as I always worked.* However, in informal speech, **like** is increasingly used for comparison of actions and conditions: *He talks fast like most salesmen do.*

as if is used in a supposed or imaginary situation, especially in formal English: *He behaves as if I were his servant.* However, in informal speech, **like** is widely tolerated in such cases: *It looks like there's been an accident.*

limerick a humorous poem of five lines. Example:
There was a young fellow named Paul
Who grew so remarkably tall
When he got into bed
By stretching his leg
He could switch off the light in the hall.

limited company a company whose shareholders have limited liability for any debts or losses of the company. More recently companies listed on the Stock Exchange describe themselves as **public limited companies (PLC)** to differentiate them from private companies **(Co Ltd)**.

literally 1 exactly in accordance with the first or most obvious meaning of what has been said: *Venice is literally sinking into the lagoon.* **2** sometimes it is used informally, with a figurative meaning, so that it means just the opposite of meaning 1: *He literally exploded when he heard the price.*

little/a little when used to express quantity: **little** suggests that there is not very much, if any: *Voodooism has little good in it, for it is based on fear*; **a little** suggests that, while there is not much, there is some: *Don't worry, I have a little money saved up*

ll lines.

LLB Bachelor of Laws.

loan see **lend**.

loathe/loath/loth: loathe to hate: *Agnes loathes water and never goes swimming.* **loath/loth** unwilling: *James was loath/loth to lend books in case they were not returned.*

lobby *politics* **1** a place in the House of Commons where people can meet Members of Parliament. **2** one of two corridors where Members of Parliament vote (sometimes called a **division lobby**). **3** a group of people who try to persuade a Member of Parliament to take an interest in their cause: *The anti-nuclear lobby persuaded their MP to raise the question of missile bases in parliament. verb* to meet an MP to influence him to take an interest in a certain cause: *A group of students went to Westminster to lobby the Education Minister about grants.*

log logarithm.

logo a special sign or symbol, used on various articles produced by a company or other organization: *His jeans had the fashionable ZOZ logo on the pocket.*

LOGO a computing language developed especially for teaching mathematics to young children. It involves giving instructions to a robot called a turtle. See **robot** and **turtle**.

long ton see **ton**.

loth see **loathe**.

lounge bar see **saloon**.

LP long-playing record.

Lr lira, lire.

Lt. Lieutenant.

luxuriant/luxurious: **luxuriant** refers to rich fertile growth usually in plants, but also in hair, feathers or fur: *luxuriant jungle undergrowth: luxuriant shining hair*. **luxurious** refers to extremely comfortable costly things: *The president's house was full of luxurious carpets*.

LW long wave.

M

m metre(s): mile(s): milli-

MA Master of Arts.

macho pronounced [matcho] describes an exaggerated pride in what are imagined to be superior masculine qualities: *Hard drinking, fighting and shooting contributed to his macho image.*

madam/madame: madam a polite term of address for a woman, often written with an initial capital letter, mainly used in shops and hotels or in formal letters. **madame** pronounced [madam] French for Mrs, and also used as a term of address. The plural of both is **mesdames** pronounced [maydam].

magic/magical: magic to do with magic: *Aladdin rubbed the magic lamp.* **magical** wonderful: *He escaped into the magical world created by the music.*

magistrate see **judge**.

mainframe computer/microcomputer: mainframe computer a very big, powerful computer able to process a large amount of information and perform a variety of complicated tasks; used in business and big organizations. **microcomputer** sometimes called **personal computer**, a much smaller, simpler machine which can be used at home or in a small business.

Maj. Major.

majority is followed by either a singular or plural verb;
plural, if thought of as a number of separate parts or
individuals: *The majority of bingo players are over
fifty;* singular, if thought of as one group: *In British
politics the majority is rarely extremely right or left
wing.*

male/masculine: male of or referring to the male sex: *a
male deer.* **masculine** describes qualities normally
associated with men rather than women: *They
recognized his heavy masculine stride down the
corridor.*

male chauvinist pig see **chauvinist.**

-man see **person.**

manoeuvre note the spelling; pronounced [**manoover**]

mark-up the amount or percentage added to the cost of
something in order to make a profit: *The mark-up on
the price of clothes may be as high as 50%.*

mathematics see **-ics.**

max. maximum.

maxi- used with other words to mean larger than
normal: *a maxi-skirt.*

may see **can.**

MBE Member of the Order of the British Empire.

MC Master of Ceremonies.

MCC Marylebone Cricket Club.

MD Doctor of Medicine.

me see **I**.

mediaeval/medieval both spellings are acceptable; the second is now commoner.

medicine note the spelling; pronounced [**medsin**] or [**medisin**].

medium 1 plural **media** newspapers, television and radio. However, **media** is now often treated as singular: *The media is responsible for the government's unpopularity.* 2 plural **mediums** a person who claims to communicate with the spirits of the dead. *The medium went into a trance and spoke with the voice of Aunt Emily who died last year.* 3 the material in which something exists or is done: *As a sculptor his medium is marble, but he also works in wood and bronze.*

Member of Parliament usually written with initial capital letters and often shortened to **MP**: *Peter went up to parliament as MP for Finchley in 1915. The majority of MPs voted in favour.*

memorandum usually shortened to **memo** 1 a note of something to remember. 2 a written statement, communication or reminder, often used instead of a letter within an organization.

Example of a memo:

MEMO   1 April 1988

To: Engineering staff

From: Works Manager's Office

The annual boiler inspection will take place or May 1st at 9 am.

memory *computers* an area inside a computer where information and instructions are stored.

menu *computers* a list of choices on a computer program.

Messrs old-fashioned plural of Mr, used eg in the addresses of formal letters.

metaphor a figure of speech in which a comparison between two people or things is implied rather than stated to produce a vivid description: *The incoming tide rummaged the shore then retreated.* An absurd impression is created however if metaphors are mixed: *On fire with enthusiasm, he sailed through the interview.*

metre, in American English **meter: 1** a measure of length in the metric system. **2** the arrangement of words in lines of poetry.

mg milligram(me)(s).

micro- used with other words to mean **1** very small: *microorganism.* **2** one millionth part: *micro millimetre.*

microchip see **chip.**

microcomputer see **mainframe computer.**

mild see **ale.**

milli- used in the metric system to indicate thousandth part of a measure: *millimetre, millilitre*

million see **billion**.

min. minimum: minute (time).

minuscule note the spelling: *The monk wrote a prayer in minuscule below the illustration in the Bible.*

minutes see **agenda**.

misc. miscellaneous.

Miss plural is **Misses**: *the Misses Bletchington*, or in less formal English, *the Miss Bletchingtons*.

mistrust see **distrust**.

ml millilitre(s): mile(s).

mm millimetre(s).

Imes Mesdames, used as *formal pl* of Mrs; see also **Madam**.

MOH Medical Officer of Health.

Mohammedan see **Moslem**.

moment: at this moment in time a fashionable expression meaning now. It is best not to overuse it.

monitor *computers* a special screen where the computer displays information. An ordinary television set is sometimes used for this purpose with a microcomputer. See also **VDU**.

moral/morale: moral *adjective* concerned with questions of right and wrong: *It would not be moral for him to have a divorce because it is against his religion. noun* **1** the lesson to be learnt from an incident or story: *The moral of the story of the boy who cried wolf is: Never ask for help unless you really need it.* **2 morals** accepted ways, standards of behaviour: *Their morals leave a lot to be desired.*

morale pronounced [mo**ral**] the state of courage or confidence of a person or group of people: *Governments often suppress bad news in wartime to keep up the nation's morale.*

mortgage pronounced [**morg**idge] a method of buying property or land with a loan repayable with interest. The lender, usually a building society or a bank, can claim the property or land if the loan is not repaid within an agreed length of time.

Moslem/Muslim/Mohammedan: Muslim is the preferred name of the followers of this religion. **Moslem** is acceptable, but **Mohammedan** is not.

MOT Ministry of Transport (often refers to a test of older motor vehicles which is required by law).

mother-in-law plural **mothers-in-law**.

motor insurance see **comprehensive insurance, third party, third party fire and theft**.

mouse *computers* a small device which can indicate in which direction a computer should move a pointer on the screen or trace graphs, or create pictures.

MP see **Member of Parliament**.

mpg, mph mile(s) per gallon, mile(s) per hour.

Ms a title substituted in writing for **Mrs** or **Miss** when the woman's status is not known or to avoid making distinctions between married and unmarried women.

MSc. Master of Science.

Mt Mount: Mountain.

municipal pronounced [myoonisipal]: *The complex of municipal buildings includes the town hall, the main library and the civic hall for public functions.*

Muslim see Moslem.

must have/must of see have.

MW medium wave.

myself it is not correct to substitute *myself* for *me*: Her presence is offensive to Mrs Whitehouse and me (not *myself*).

N

National Savings Bank a bank run by the UK government, through post offices, which gives small savers with ordinary accounts a low rate of interest tax-free up to a certain amount per year. Its investment accounts have a high rate of interest but they are taxed.

National Savings Certificate a document issued to investors in Government securities, an un-complicated method of saving which, with tax-free interest, is attractive to the small investor.

NATO North Atlantic Treaty Organization.

naught/nought: **naught** old-fashioned term for nothing: *Long John's evil plan came to naught.* **nought** the figure 0: *Let's play noughts and crosses.*

NB note well, an abbreviation of Latin *nota bene*, used to bring something to the attention of the reader: *NB The prices quoted in the above list do not apply to the Irish Republic.*

NCO non-commissioned officer.

née means born and is used to indicate the surname of a married woman before her marriage: *Mrs Celia Good, née Smith.*

negative double negatives are fairly common in speech

but are not acceptable: *Poor Mr Archer never had no luck.* should be: *Poor Mr Archer never had any luck.*

negligent/negligible: negligent refers to a lack of proper care and attention: *When my new car broke down, I was able to claim a replacement because the manufacturers had been negligent.*

negligible refers to something too small or unimportant to be considered: *There is no point in travelling to Rome by train rather than by air, because the difference in cost is negligible.*

negro/black both are used to refer to people of African race, but as **negro** is commonly felt to be offensive, **black** is preferable.

neither meaning not the one . . . not the other, is followed by a singular verb: *Neither of the twins is tall.*

neither/nor the form of the verb depends on the noun which follows **nor**: *Neither you nor Jane is very fat. Neither Jews nor Moslims eat pork.* The exception to this is when the noun after **neither** is plural, but the noun after **nor** is singular: *Neither the shoes nor the hat suit her.*

neo- combines with words to indicate that the original has been revived in an altered form: *neo-Nazi, neo-classical: Recently built houses often have neo-Georgian window frames with a modern type of glass.*

net/nett refers to something, especially money or weight, to which nothing is to be added or taken away: *After tax deductions, Tom earns £12 000 net.*

Both spellings are acceptable.

never did not ... ever: *Shakespeare never went to Italy although he wrote about it.* The use of **never** to mean simply did not is widespread and acceptable in informal language. *Liar! I never touched your money.*

NHS National Health Service.

nitty-gritty in informal English, the practical but unpleasant details which have to be faced: *To get down to the nitty-gritty, who's paying for the council's splendid schemes?*

no claims bonus the discount which an insurance company allows to a client on his annual payment for a car insurance if he has made no claims for a number of years: *Henry had two car accidents this year and lost his no claims bonus.*

none can be followed by a singular or plural verb. When it refers to a mass or bulk a singular verb is used: *None of the water is contaminated.* When it refers to a group considered as a whole, the verb is plural: *None of the gang ever have any money.* But if the individuals who make up the group are emphasized the verb is singular: *All pupils must wear uniform, none of you is excluded.*

non-flammable see **flammable**.

nor see **neither**.

north/south/east/west the points of the compass are

usually written with a small initial letter, except when they are part of a name or used as a name. *The west of the country is mountainous. These birds are found in northern regions.* BUT *South America; North Yorkshire. They live in the West Country* (meaning the west of England).

Compounds are usually hyphenated: *north-east; west-south-west; South-East Asia.*

When abbreviated, north, south, east and west are always written with capital letters, usually without full stops: *N, NE, WSW.*

North America see **America**.

Northern Ireland see **Britain** and **Eire**.

nought see **naught**.

noun a word which tells what a person, thing or quality is: the *girl*; a *fall* of rain; *honesty*. These are all **common nouns**. A **proper noun**, usually written with an initial capital letter, is the name of an individual person, place or organization etc: *Mary; Robert; London.*

no way not at all: *I can't lend you £10. No way!* This fairly new usage is quite acceptable in informal speech if it is not overused.

nr near.

NT New Testament.

number of note that with **a number of** a plural verb is used: *A number of cigarette ends have been found behind the cycle sheds.* However, with **the number of,**

a singular verb is used: *The number of smokers has decreased.* See also **amount**.

NY New York.

O

OAP Old Age Pensioner.

o/oh: O expresses surprise or strong emotion in poetry or song, usually when addressing someone or something: *O dearest love.* **Oh** is the more modern way to represent this speech sound: *Oh, I've lost my ticket.*

OBE Officer of the Order of the British Empire.

object see **subject**.

oblivious meaning not aware can be followed by **of** or by: *He went on banging the drum quite oblivious to (of) the neighbour's protests.*

observation/observance: observation 1 taking notice, noticing or watching: *The police kept the house under close observation after twenty people entered carrying sacks.* **2** a remark: *She made a few observations about the weather, then fell silent.*

   observance performing or keeping to a ritual, ceremony, custom etc: *Mrs Clark insisted on strict observance of Sunday, beginning with family prayers and then morning service at church.*

obsolete/obsolescent: obsolete gone out of use, out of date: *Aeroplanes which became obsolete after World War II are sometimes kept in museums.*

obsolescent going out of use, becoming out of date: *It's a good idea to keep obsolescent tools as they may become valuable antiques in the future.*

occasion/occasional note the spelling: *We went out for an occasional drink at the local.*

occidental/oriental: occidental means Western and refers to the countries of Europe and the USA as opposed to those of the east. **oriental** means Eastern and refers to the countries of Asia or the Eastern Mediterranean.

occur note the spelling: **occurred, occurring:** *The incident occurred on a Friday afternoon.*

of/'s to show possession: it is possible to use either **of** or **'s** with a large number of nouns: *the river's murky water* or *the murky water of the river*. In the case of people, animals, time and names of places, **'s** is normally used: *Pandora's box, the cat's paw, in a week's time, Ireland's population*. Beyond this it is hard to give definite rules.

official/officious: official approved of by the proper authority: *Everyone says there will be an election soon, but it is not official until the Prime Minister announces the date.* **officious** giving advice, help etc where it is unwanted or not needed, interfering: *Our officious neighbour called to remind us that we had not cut the lawn for three weeks.*

offline see **online.**

OHMS On Her/His Majesty's Service.

OK informal way of saying 'all right'.

older/oldest see **elder/eldest**.

O-level the lower level of the GCE, usually taken by 5th year secondary-school pupils before 1987, when it was replaced by the GCSE in England, Wales and Northern Ireland. See **GCE** and **A-level**.

omelet/omelette both spellings are acceptable; pronounced [**om**lit].

on see **upon**.

one an indefinite person: *One can find every kind of shop in London.* This pronoun is best confined to formal, literary or technical language for two reasons: **1** if **one** is used in a sentence the speaker must continue with **one** and **one's** (in British English) which can cause confusion or sound clumsy: *One likes to arrange one's room in one's own way.* **2 one** can seem arrogant or affected so that it is better to use **you**: *You like to arrange your room in your own way.*

one another see **each other**.

online/offline *computers* refer to such devices as disk drives or cassette recorders used with a computer: **online** means that the equipment is ready to be used; **offline** means that it is switched off or disconnected.

only the position of **only** can change the meaning of a sentence: *Only you can make me happy* (nobody else can). *Bernard only borrowed your car* (he did not steal it). *Cleo confides only in me* (she confides in nobody else).

ono or nearest offer. See **advertisement**.

onto/on to both are correct when **on** means in or to a certain position: *Put it onto (on to) the table.* But when **on** means further or forward, always use **on to**: *I am going on to London.*

onward/onwards *adverb* both forms are possible: *Let us hurry onward (onwards) to our final goal.* *adjective* only **onward** is used: *An onward movement of the vehicles showed that the road was clear.*

OPEC Organization of Petroleum Exporting Countries.

open cheque see **cheque**.

open punctuation see **letters**.

oral/aural both pronounced [oral] but **oral** means spoken or given through the mouth: *oral medicine. Jenny gets tongue-tied in oral exams.* **aural** concerns the ear or hearing: *I find it hard to concentrate on listening in aural exams.*

ordinary shares see **stocks and shares**.

oriental see **occidental**.

orthopaedics/orthopedics both spellings are acceptable; the branch of medicine dealing with bones and joints.

OT Old Testament.

ght not/didn't ought: ought not is the only acceptable form although **didn't ought** can be heard frequently in informal speech.

tdoor/outdoors/out of doors: outdoor is an adjective to describe something outside: *Canoeing is an outdoor activity.* **outdoors** and **out of doors** are adverbial: *Wear boots if you go outdoors (out of doors) in the snow.*

tput *computers* any information which a computer gives the user.

erdraft the amount of money owing to a bank when a customer, with the permission of the bank manager, withdraws more money than he actually has in his account: *When we bought our new car, Fred had to ask for an overdraft as it cost £1 000 more than we expected.*

erdrawn having withdrawn more money than one actually has in one's bank account (usually without the permission of the bank manager): *The bank manager asked me to transfer money from my deposit account to my current account as the latter was overdrawn.*

erly too, excessively: *Jim's mother is overly protective.* This usage has not been completely accepted in British usage.

ing to see **due to**.

bridge the universities of Oxford and Cambridge considered together as centres of high academic

achievement, as opposed to the more moder
universities. Compare **redbrick**.

OXFAM Oxford Committee for Famine Relief.

Oxford English pronunciation of English thought of
setting a standard of correctness. See also **Queen**
English, BBC English, standard English.

P

penny: p is the written symbol and the informal name for one penny; the plural is **p's:** *Can you give me ten 1p's for a 10p coin?* The plural of **penny** is **pennies** or **pence.** Although **one pence** is not logical, it is acceptable in everyday speech. In old British money, before 1972, the abbreviation for **penny** was **d** (from Latin *denarius*).

a. per annum.

ediatrics/pediatrics both spellings are acceptable; the branch of medicine dealing with children's illnesses.

jamas/pyjamas both spellings are acceptable.

and p. postage and packing.

r(a) paragraph.

ra- used with other words to mean beside, near; beyond; resembling, very like: *paramedical; parallel; paramilitary.*

raffin note the spelling. *Paraffin lamps used to be a common form of lighting.*

ragraph usually indented or started a little way in rom the margin. See **letters** for methods of aragraphing business letters.

parallel note the spelling: *the parallel lines of the ra*
track.

paralyse/paralysis note the spelling: *The accident le*
him paralysed from the waist down.

parameter something which limits a project, schem
etc: *The town planners have to work within certai*
parameters as far as money and time are concerne
as cheap housing is needed quickly.

parentheses see **brackets**.

parliament pronounced [**par**liment], though a fe
people like to say [**par**lyament].

partially/partly both mean not completely: *When th*
got to the hotel, they found it was only part
(partially) finished and the rooms were witho
doors.

participles forms of the verb which end in *-ing*, *-ed*, ·
They are used to form certain verbs:
    present participle ends in *-ing*: *I was sailing do*
river.
    past participle ends in *-ed*, *-d*, *-t*, *-n* etc: *She return*
cut, bruised and shaken.
    Participles can also be used as follows: *Listening*
Bill's evidence, I detected no signs of remor.
Tempted by the smell, the beast moved nearer to ·
trap. Participles used in this way must refer to t
subject of the main clause; otherwise the effect
ridiculous: *Repairing the car, a stray dog knocked* ·
oil can over.

Pascal a computer language which can be used for scientific, technical and commercial subjects. It can deal with both simple and complex problems in an economical way.

passed/past: passed is simply the past tense and past participle of the verb to pass: *He passed me the pepper instead of the salt.* past *adverb: They walked past the window without looking in.* past *adjective: On past occasions few people have attended these meetings.* past *noun: In the past people wrote on slates.* See also participles.

past participle see participles.

PAYE Pay As You Earn (Income Tax).

PC Police Constable; Privy Councillor; personal computer.

pc postcard.

pd paid.

PE physical education.

pediatrics see paediatrics.

penny see p.

people see person.

perennial see annual.

period see full stop.

peripheral *computers* any piece of equipment which can be connected to a computer, such as a cassette recorder, disk drive or printer.

perk used informally for **perquisite** anything gained legally in payment for work done apart from or in addition to money: *One of the perks of his job in the brewery is free beer.*

person plural **people**, also **persons** in legal or formal contexts: *Any persons entering this building do so at their own risk.* **-person** is now often substituted for **-man** to reflect sexual equality: *Wanted experienced ploughperson.* This can be a useful indication of attitudes but if taken to extremes, can be absurd as with *huperson* for *human being.*

    people can also be used in the singular to mean the people of a country or other cultural group: *the peoples of Central America.*

personal/personnel: personal private, individual: *Her personal notepaper has the family coat of arms on it.* **personnel** 1 the group of people employed in the same factory or institution, followed by a plural verb: *Laboratory personnel are required to wear gloves.* 2 informal short form of **personnel department** the department in a large company or other organization which deals with matters concerning the staff: *Take those forms up to personnel.*

personal computer see **mainframe computer**.

perverse/perverted: perverse deliberately going against what is reasonable or appropriate: *The perverse child refuses to eat at mealtimes and cries for food as soon as she is in bed.* **perverted** refers someone or something turned away from what is right, good or natural: *Someone with a perverted sense of humour has let down the tyres of the invalid car.*

pharmaceutical note the spelling; pronounced [farmasyootical]: *The pharmaceutical industries spend too much on promotion of drugs and not enough on research.*

PhD Doctor of Philosophy.

phlegm note the spelling; pronounced [flem]: *He cleared the phlegm from his throat.*

picnic note the spelling: **picknicked, picknicking**: *They picknicked by the seashore.*

pitiful/piteous both words mean deserving pity, though **pitiful** is more usual in everyday speech: *The kitten's pitiful (piteous) cries led the boys to the chimney where it was trapped.* **pitiful** also refers to a person or thing so feeble or bad that they deserve contempt: *What a pitiful floral display there was, with all the tulips wilting and weeds everywhere.*

plaid Cymry pronounced [plyde **koomry**] the Welsh Nationalist Party, aiming at home rule for Wales.

plain/plane *nouns* **plain** a level stretch of countryside: *There are only three or four big hills in the Cheshire plain.* **plane** 1 a tool for levelling and smoothing wood: *After Jim got a splinter in his hand he smoothed the shelf with a plane.* 2 a flat surface. 3 a level: *They kept the discussion on an informal plane.*

4 short for aeroplane. **5** a plane tree: *Many London parks have plane trees.*

plait pronounced [plat]: *In those days we all wore our hair in plaits.*

PLC see **limited company**.

plotter *computers* a device which uses signals from a computer to draw graphs, diagrams and pictures and print them out onto paper.

P.M. 1 also **p.m.** abbreviation for Latin *post meridiem* the period of time between midday and midnight **2** usually **PM** abbreviation for Prime Minister.

pneumatic note the spelling; pronounced [newmatic] worked by or containing air pressure: *They were digging up the road all day with a pneumatic drill.*

pneumonia note the spelling; pronounced [newmonia] a serious infection of the lungs.

PO Post Office; postal order; Petty Officer; Pilot Officer

POB/PO Box abbreviations of **Post Office Box** a private numbered place in a post office where people may have their mail sent instead of to their address

policy a document containing a contract of insurance issued by an insurance company to a client.

pop population.

pore see **pour**.

portfolio *finance* the range of financial investment

held by an individual, or an institution such as an insurance company or a pension fund.

possessive pronoun see pronoun.

postcard only the bare essentials need be included: the name and address of the person to whom it is sent, the date, a brief message and the signature of the sender.

example of a postcard:

23 7 88

Have now arrived
safely in Paris
Weather could be
better but we are
enjoying the break.
Thanks for all
your help.
With best wishes,
Jane

Mrs. M. Brown
54 Top Street
OCKLES
Cheshire CW0 0AB
England

poste restante an address which can be put on letters and parcels if they are to stay at a post office until they are collected. This system is often used by people who have no definite address in a town or who are simply passing through: *Elaine is touring Spain, so send her letters 'Poste Restante, Madrid'.*

Post Office Box see **POB**.

pour/pore: pour to cause liquid to flow out: *Tim poured himself a glass of gin.* **pore** to study or examine something very intently: *The professor pored over the ancient manuscripts until his eyes were tired.*

POW prisoner of war.

pp pages; on behalf of/for (used when a secretary or another person signs a letter for someone else with their permission).

PR public relations.

practicable/practical both mean able to function or be carried out, but: **practical** has an extra suggestion of efficient or sensible: *We could use candles to light the office, but it would not be practical in modern times. They did a trial run to see if the plan was practicable.*

practice/practise: practice is a noun: *Ted loathes piano practice.* **practise** is a verb: *Ted practises his piano pieces every day.*

precede/proceed: both words are rather formal. **precede** to go before: *The Queen preceded the*

Princess in the procession. **proceed** to move forward, continue: *The trial proceeded after the break for lunch.*

précis note the spelling; pronounced [**praysee**] a summary: *The students made a précis of the novel in order to analyse the story.*

refer note the spelling: **preferred, preferring:** *He preferred his first school to his second.*

reference shares see **stocks and shares.**

refix a word or syllable placed before another word or syllable to change its meaning: *ex-* (ex-army); *anti-* (anti-American). Recent prefixes tend to be joined on with a hyphen, but older ones are written as part of the word: *exorbitant; anticipate.* Compare **suffix.**

remium a payment made to an insurance company for insurance.

remium bond also called **premium savings bond** a numbered bond issued by the UK government as part of a kind of lottery scheme. No interest is paid on the bond but prizes are given each month to the owners of the bonds whose numbers are drawn. Each bond is worth £1, they are sold in blocks of £5, and prizes range from £5 to £100 000.

reposition a word which is followed by a noun or pronoun and which shows how that word is related to others, eg in terms of place: *The book is on the table*; time: *He came after the party*; state or condition: *Tell me about it.*

prescribe/proscribe: prescribe of a doctor, to recommend the use of something: *The doctor prescribed calamine lotion for the baby's rash.* **proscribe 1** to forbid something. **2** to condemn or banish someone as a criminal: *Robin Hood was proscribed by the Sheriff of Nottingham.*

premise/premiss 1 both spellings are acceptable; a statement that is assumed to be true so that by accepting it one can come to a conclusion about something else: *If we take as our first premiss that the poor are unhealthy, then the government must tackle the causes of poverty as well as ill health.* **2 premises** a building or buildings with surroundings: *The thieves were discovered on the premises.*

Pres. President.

present participle see **participles**.

pressure group a group of people acting together to publicize their aims and persuade influential people to support them: *Pressure groups caused the government to drop plans for a new airport.* Compare **ginger group**.

presume see **assume**.

primarily pronounced [**primerily**].

principal/principle: principal *adjective* most important: *The principal language in Britain is English.* *noun* the head of an institution or company. **principle** a fundamental theory or rule: *It was again Grandma's principles to refuse hospitality.*

printer *computers* a piece of equipment which can print information from the computer's memory on to paper. See **daisy wheel** and **dot-matrix**.

print-out *computers* the output of a computer printed on paper, sometimes also called **hard copy**.

privilege note the spelling: *Hetty was a privileged child whose parents bought her the best piano available.*

PRO public relations officer; Public Record Office.

pro. professional.

prob. probably.

probate 1 the process of proving that a will is genuine. **2** the official document from the High Court which executors of a will must get to show that they have a legal right to deal with the dead person's property and money. Note that if the dead person has not left a will, his or her representatives must get a grant of **letters of administration** from the High Court. See **will**.

proceed see **precede**.

prodigy/protégé: prodigy 1 an unusually talented person, often a child: *Nicholas was a child prodigy and went to University at the age of twelve.* **2** a wonderful or wonderful or wonderful event or thing. **protégé** pronounced [**prot**ayzhay] a person who is protected and helped by a more powerful and influential person: *Rita was a protégé of Lady Bunbury who had great faith in her future as a fashion designer.*

professor note the spelling; in Britain a senior member

of a university department, in America, a university lecturer. Sometimes shortened to **Prof.**

program/programme the normal British spelling is **programme**, the American spelling is **program**. In technical computer language however the spelling is always **program**, meaning the list of instructions to a computer which tell it how to perform a particular task.

pronoun a word used in place of a noun: *I* saw *them. She* met *us.*

An **interrogative pronoun** asks a question: *Which* of you has a pen? *Who* said that?

A **relative pronoun** introduces a new part of a sentence: This is the boy *who* came first. The books *which* you like are over there. See also **that.**

A **possessive pronoun** shows possession belonging: That book is *mine.* It's not *hers.*

proper noun see **noun.**

prophecy/prophesy: prophecy is a noun: *Macbeth listened to the prophecy of the witches.* **prophesy** is a verb: *He prophesied that Jerusalem would be destroyed.*

proscribe see **prescribe.**

prostate/prostrate: prostate a gland in males near the neck of the bladder: *He had an operation on his prostate gland.* **prostrate 1** lying face downwards a sign of absolute humility: *The servants of the*

Ethiopian prince remained prostrate at his feet.
2 utterly exhausted: *Three tragic deaths in the family left the others prostrate with grief.* **3** completely helpless: *The people were prostrate before the cruelty and oppression of Amin and his soldiers.*

Prot. Protestant.

proto-/prot- both are used with other words to mean: **1** first in time, order or rank: *proto-history* (the first stage of history before people began to use writing). **2** the original form of something: *prototype* (an original model on which future copies are based).

PS postscript.

pseudonym note the spelling; pronounced [syoodonim] a fictitious name used by an author: *Charles Dickens used the pseudonym Boz.*

psychology/psychiatry note the spelling: **psychology** the scientific study of the mind and of human and animal behaviour. **psychiatry** the branch of medicine dealing with the study and treatment of mental disorders.

psychopath a person with a mental disorder who does violent and antisocial things with no feelings of guilt: *Hitler has often been called a psychopath.*

psychosomatic note the spelling; refers to illness thought to be caused by stress or mental disorders rather than physical problems: *We think John's diarrhoea is psychosomatic because he always has attacks before he has to deal with complaints.*

PT physical training.

pt pint(s).

PTA Parent-Teacher Association.

Pte. Private (in the British army).

PTO please turn over.

public bar see salon.

public limited company see limited company.

punctuation see apostrophe, brackets, colon, comma, dash, exclamation marks, full stop, hyphen, question marks, quotations marks, semi-colon. For open and closed punctuation see letters.

PVC polyvinyl chloride (a kind of plastic).

pyjamas see pajamas.

Q

QC Queen's Counsel, high-ranking barrister or advocate.

qr quarter(s).

quango short for quasi autonomous non-governmental organization, a body financed by the government but not controlled by it, set up to investigate and develop questions of national interest: *The Countryside Commission is a quango.*

quasi- pronounced [**kwayz**eye] combines with other words to mean virtually: *The Sisterhood is a quasi-religious community dedicated to meditation.*

Queen's English (or **King's English** when the monarch is a man) an informal name for standard English. *That's not the Queen's English.* See **standard English**.

question mark symbol used: **1** before every question which needs a separate answer. *Who's that? What's happening?* **2** before any item one is doubtful about: *Zol Hines, born 1809 died (?) 1856.*

questionnaire note the spelling; pronounced [kwesty**onare**] or [kesty**onare**]: *They sent out questionnaires to find out which brands people preferred.*

quit the past is **quit** or **quitted**: *She quit (quitted) her job when the new manager arrived.*

quotation marks (also known as **inverted commas**) both single and double are used, but single are becoming commoner. They are used:

1 to mark the actual words of a speaker or writer. There are some rules to follow:

(1) All punctuation marks which are part of the quotation go inside the quotation marks; thus if the speaker is asking a question the question mark is before the final quotation mark: *'Who are you?' gasped Edna.* At the end of a quotation and before such phrases as *he said* the comma is placed before the quotation marks: *'I feel ill,' he moaned.*

(2) For a quotation within a quotation double commas are used: *'Did he really say "Go to hell" to the headmaster?' asked Eileen.*

(3) Where a phrase such as *he said* comes in the middle of an incomplete sentence, the comma is placed thus: *'You', she hissed, 'are an interfering little busybody.'*

2 to indicate that a word or phrase is in some way special because it is slang or foreign etc: *Why did Justin 'bash you' as you put it?*

For titles of poems etc see **titles of works**.

R

R registered trade mark.

RA Royal Academy.

RAC Royal Automobile Club.

rabies/rabid: rabies *noun* an infectious disease causing madness in dogs and other animals. People can be infected with it from the bite of a rabid dog. **rabid 1** suffering from rabies: *The rabid dog staggered down the street until a man shot it.* **2** expressing extreme or violent ideas, especially political views: *For years Tom was a rabid fascist and an admirer of Hitler but a visit to Berlin in 1940 changed his views.*

racial/racialist/racist all three relate to the division of the human race into distinct groups according to physical characteristics: *Straight black hair is a racial characteristic of Chinese and Japanese people.* However, **racialist** and **racist** are concerned with the belief that some races are inferior to others: *Many libraries are actively trying to exclude racist (racialist) literature and encourage multicultural attitudes.*

RADA Royal Academy of Dramatic Art.

radius plural **radii** pronounced [radieye]: the length of a straight line from the centre of a circle to its outside edge. *The radii of these circles are equal.*

RAF Royal Air Force.

RAM *computers* abbreviation of **random access memory** The memory available to the user for putting in and taking out information. This can be erased and when the computer is switched off the information is usually lost. It is commonly used as a measure of the computer's capacity: *This program uses 512K of RAM.* Compare **ROM**.

RC Roman Catholic.

Rd Road: rand(s).

RE religious education.

re- see **hyphen**.

recd received.

ref. reference.

receipt note the spelling. *Luckily Bill was able to show his receipt to the store detective who accused him of stealing a tin of cocoa.*

recommend/recommendation note the spelling: *This hotel was recommended to us by our neighbour.*

reconnaissance note the spelling; pronounced [rekonesans]: *The soldiers went out on reconnaissance to find out the enemy's position.*

recorded delivery a post-office service by which the sender gets official proof of posting and of delivery for an extra charge. Compare **registered post**.

recourse see **resort**.

rector/vicar: in the Church of England, both nowadays are clergymen in charge of a parish. The history of the parish determines which title is used now. In former times a parish could have a **rector** who had rights to all the tithes paid, or a **vicar**, who had no such rights, to take the rector's place.

redbrick describes British universities founded in the nineteenth and early twentieth centuries as distinct from Oxford and Cambridge. See **Oxbridge**.

referee in an application for a job, a person who is willing to give information about the character, abilities etc of an applicant for a job. The names and addresses of at least two such people should be included in a curriculum vitae and their position should be made clear. See **curriculum vitae**.

reference, reference number see **letters**.

regal/royal both describe matters related to kings and queens. **regal** like or fit for a king: *The old headmistress had such a regal bearing that she was referred to as Her Majesty.* **royal 1** from or concerning a king or queen: *During the royal tour of China Queen Elizabeth saw the Great Wall.* **2** fit for a king: *The footballers were given a royal welcome by their fans.*

regarding/with regard to/in regard to/as regards all mean about, in connection with: *As regards your* *enquiry about taxation, I enclose an information leaflet.* Such expressions are formal and often used in letters.

registered post a post-office service by which the sender, for an extra charge, gets official proof of posting and delivery, and compensation is paid if the contents of the letter or parcel are lost or damaged. Compare **recorded delivery**.

relation/relative both are acceptable meaning a member of one's family.

relatively in comparison with something else: *In Britain apples are relatively cheap (compared with pineapples).*

rent see **hire**.

repertoire/repertory: repertoire in music or the theatre, the collection of works available to be performed: *They have a fine repertoire of French songs.* **repertory** sometimes shortened in informal speech to **rep** a system in the theatre whereby different plays are performed in turn by the same company in the same season: *Twelfth Night is now in repertory in Stratford. She acted for three years in repertory theatre.*

reply see **letters, invitations**.

republican/Republican: republican of a republic; supporting government by a republic (rather than by a monarch). **Republican** a member or supporter of the Republican party, one of the two main political parties of the USA. Compare **democrat**.

resort to/have recourse to: both mean to use something as a source of help, usually because other means have failed: *Henry must have his own way even if it means resorting to dishonest means.*

especting/with respect to/in respect of very formal or legal expressions for about or concerning: *The judge spoke to the jury with respect to the tender age of the accused.*

esuscitate note the spelling: *We thought the man was dead but the ambulance driver managed to resuscitate him with the kiss of life.*

etd retired.

etro- used with other words to mean backwards; back; behind: *retrospect (looking back).*

Rev., Revd. Reverend (see **titles** under **letters**).

evenge see **avenge**.

eview/revue: review a critical article, an assessment: *The Morning Post had a review of her new book. Around New Year, there is a television review of the events of the previous twelve months.* **revue** a comic theatrical show consisting of several separate sections: *The Cambridge Footlights Revue.*

hyme/rhythm note the spelling.

I religious instruction.

ght-wing *politics* describes the more conservative

views of people who tend to be against fundamental social change.

RIP may he/she rest in peace (in Latin *requiescat in pace*).

RN Royal Navy.

robot *computers* a machine controlled by a computer to work in a set way. It is used to do jobs which are dangerous, tiring or time-consuming for people, such as welding car bodies in a factory.

robotics *computers* the use of computers and modern technology to control machinery especially in complex manufacturing processes which formerly required a large skilled workforce: *Robotics expert invented a device which could work in levels of heat that humans could not stand.*

ROM *computers* abbreviation of **read only memory** that part of the computer's memory which cannot be erased, where the operating instructions are stored. Compare **RAM**.

Roman numerals see **arabic** (under **Arab**).

round brackets see **brackets**.

royal see **regal**.

RSM Regimental Sergeant Major.

RSPB Royal Society for the Protection of Birds.

RSPCA Royal Society for the Prevention of Cruelty to Animals.

RSPCC Royal Society for the Prevention of Cruelty to Children.

RSVP see invitations.

Rt. Hon. Right Honourable.

S

's see **of**.

saccharin/saccharine note the spelling: **saccharin** pronounced [sakarin] *noun* a very sweet substance used as a substitute for sugar: *Karen puts saccharin in her tea.* **saccharine** pronounced [sakareen] *adjective* too sweet, very sweet: *Gladys spoke in a saccharine tone which to me was a sign of insincerity.*

sae stamped addressed envelope.

salable/saleable both spellings are acceptable: *After a few days in the shop most fruit is no longer salable (saleable) and should now be thrown out.*

salon/saloon: salon 1 a place where eg a hairdresser carries on business. *They have two salons in the city centre.* **2** in former times, a meeting, especially of writers and artists, in a fashionable private house: *Madame Récamier often held a salon in Paris.* **saloon 1** a large public sitting room on a ship. **2** also **saloon bar** or **lounge bar** a bar which is more comfortable and where drinks cost more than in a **public bar**.

SALT abbreviation of **strategic arms limitation talks**.

sapphire note the spelling.

sarcasm see **irony**.

sauna pronounced [**saw**na] or [**sow**na] a kind of Finnish steam-bath.

sauté pronounced [**so**tay]; the past is **sautéd** [**so**tayd] to fry vegetables lightly: *fish with sautéd potatoes.*

save *computers* to record a program or data from a computer onto a disk or cassette recorder.

savings account see **account.**

savoury/savory: savoury, in American English **savory,** tasting good; having a non-sweet taste: *We prefer savoury to sweet dishes.* Also used as a noun: *They always serve savouries at their parties.* **savory** is also the name of a herb used in cooking, especially in meat dishes.

SCE see **GCE.**

scenario/scene are both concerned with the action in a play or film.

scene is the unit of action or the place where it happens: *Scene 3 London Bridge.*

scenario 1 an outline of the plot and characters. **2** outside the theatre and cinema, an imagined version of events: *The peace campaigner described a scenario in which a crazy dictator could start a nuclear war.*

sceptical see **cynical.**

schedule note the spelling: pronounced [**shed**yool] in British English and [**sked**yool] in American English: *We asked the builder to draw up a schedule for the whole building process so that we could get a better* *idea of when it would be finished.*

sci fi science fiction.

sciatica pronounced [siatica] pain in the thighs, hips, lower back.

Scotch/Scottish/Scots all describe the people and things of Scotland but: **Scottish** and **Scots** are preferred in Scotland: *Scottish politics, Scottish schools* but *Scots law, the Scots language;* **Scotch** is now used mainly in certain compounds: *Scotch terrier,* many of them referring to food and drink: *Scotch whisky, Scotch broth.*

Scottish National Party the political party in favour of home rule for Scotland. Sometimes shortened to SNP.

screen *computers* see **monitor**.

SDP see **Social Democratic Party**.

seasonal/seasonable: seasonal depending on the time of year, changing with the seasons: *The tourist trade is seasonal with a very busy period in summer and less busy time in spring and autumn.*

   seasonable 1 happening at the right season: *A seasonable frost lay on the ground as the Christmas carols began.* **2** coming at the right time: *A seasonable gift of money came from Grandpa at the start of the holidays.*

Sec., Secy Secretary.

second the adjective and noun are pronounced

[second]: *Wait a second. That's the second time you've let me down.* The verb is pronounced [second]: *He was seconded to another department for three months to help out, on condition that he would then return to his own section.*

second name see **family name**.

second person the grammatical form of pronouns and verbs when they refer to the person being spoken to: *you* is the second person pronoun (singular and plural). See also **first person** and **third person**.

securities see **stocks and shares**.

semantic refers to the meaning of words and symbols: *Red traffic lights and the word 'stop' carry the same semantic message.*

semi- (from Latin; compare **hemi-**) used with other words to mean half: *semitone.*

semi-blocked business letter see **letter**.

semi-colon marks a pause in a sentence, stronger than a comma, but weaker than a full stop:

   1 it is used in much the same way as words like *and* or *but*: *Children start projects with enthusiasm; they finish them with reluctance.*

   2 it separates lists into subdivisions: *The main sources of income are from the mining, distributing and selling of salt; the rearing, milking and breeding of cattle; garment manufacturing.*

SEN State Enrolled Nurse.

Sen. Senator: senior.

sensual/sensuous both describe things related to physical sensations but: **sensuous** tends simply to describe pleasure: *The dancers delighted in beautiful sensuous movement.* **sensual** often carries condemnation: *The writer was criticized for stressing the sensual aspects of love at the expense of spiritual and moral values.*

separate note the spelling.

sexist refers to unfair treatment based on sex, particularly where men discriminate against women: *Women drivers are the subject of sexist jokes.*

SF science fiction.

Sgt. Sergeant.

shall/will are used to express:
1 the future;
2 determination, obligation.

Use of the two words is varied, depending on the age of the user, the region, whether the language is formal or informal. The two formerly considered the main correct uses and still widely used are:

	future	determination/ obligation
I/we	shall	will
you, he, she, it, they	will	shall

He will be ten tomorrow. You shall die for this!

However, it is acceptable and very common to use *will* for all persons: *I will go with you and together we will win through.*

shammy see **chamois**.

shares see **stocks and shares**.

sheikh pronounced [shake].

short ton see **ton**.

should/would can both be used with *I* and *we* in the following cases:

   1 in reported speech: *'I know I shall lose it!' 'I knew I should (would) lose it.'*

   2 in conditional sentences such as: *I should (would) sell it, if I were you. We should (would) help if we could.*

   3 in polite requests: *I should (would) like a double whisky please.* The modern preference is for *would*, especially in informal speech and writing.

   should is used to express the following:

   1 ought to: *David should feed the cat.*

   2 possibility: *The key should be around somewhere.*

   3 doubt, unlikely condition etc: *They saved the money until they should need it. It is odd he should be so tired. If we should need help, we'll ask Uncle Gus. The police took care he should not escape.*

   would is used to express the following:

   1 a form of the past tense: *People would make their own entertainment in the old days.*

   2 willingness: *I would gladly help you.*

    3 insistence: *Stephen would slam the door.*
    4 possibility: *A black labrador? That would be our neighbour's dog.*

    should (would) have liked/should (would) like to have both are acceptable: *I should (would) have liked to see their new baby. We should (would) like to have spoken to the headmaster.*

SI in French *Système Internationale (d'Unités)* international system of units (of measurement based on the metre etc).

signature see **letters**.

silicon/silicone: silicon a very common element and the main constituent of sand and rock. A small slice of silicon is used to make a microchip, the main functional part of a computer. (See **microchip** under **chip**). **silicone** a compound of silicon used especially in lubricants and water repellents.

simile pronounced [simily] a figure of speech in which one thing is compared to another: *Her hair is like straw.*

simplistic 1 extremely simple or naive: *People are either good and will go to heaven or bad and will go to hell, according to Auntie Freda's simplistic views.*
2 unrealistic, oversimplifying complicated problems: *Ted's simplistic solution to overproduction at the factory was to pay the workers to stay at home.*

sincerely: Yours sincerely see **letters**.

Sinn Fein pronounced [shin **fane**] a republican Irish

political movement and party.

sister-in-law plural **sisters-in-law**.

ski note the spelling: **skied; skiing**.

skilful note the spelling.

slander/libel both are legal terms for offences in which statements are made which are damaging to a person's reputation, but **slander** refers to something spoken and **libel** to something written.

slang words and phrases commonly used in conversation, but not acceptable on more formal occasions or in writing, and often used by particular groups of people. After a time they tend to become unfashionable or else to become an acceptable part of the language: *'Clear off and peel the spuds,' she yelled, unexpectedly using the slang his friends spoke in the street.*

Sloane Ranger slang name for a young Londoner (usually a woman) who is rich, confident, keen on sport and animals and expensively but informally dressed.

slush fund money set aside to be used for dishonest purposes in politics, such as bribery.

smell the past is **smelt** or **smelled**; **smelt** is commoner.

SNP see **Scottish National Party**.

Soc. Society.

so-called 1 refers to something that has no right to be

described in a certain way: *Some so-called meat stew* *contain no meat at all.* 2 refers to something as it i called in technical language: *Doctor Dopp spok about the so-called Gloucestershire disease.*

Social Democratic Party a fairly new major politica party in the UK, often called the **SDP**. Its views ar neither extremely right- nor left-wing and it is allie with the Liberal Party (see **Liberal Party**).

Socialist see **Labour Party**.

social security/social service/social work: socia security money paid by the government to help thos in need, eg the old, the sick, the unemployed: *He wa on social security for six months before he found job.* **social service** any of the services paid for by th government, partly from taxes, eg health, polic education. **social work** work done to help those i need, especially if paid for by the government.

soft drugs see **hard drugs**.

soft porn see **hard porn**.

software see **hardware**.

softwood see **hardwood**.

solicitor see **barrister**.

somebody/someone both are correct.

son-in-law plural **sons-in-law**.

south see **north**.

speciality/specialty both are acceptable, but the latt

is commoner in Scottish and North American English.

specially see **especially**.

sperm bank a deep-frozen store of sperm which is kept in certain clinics for the fertilization of women whose partners are impotent or who are without partners.

spill past is **spilt** or **spilled**; **spilt** is commoner.

split infinitive an infinitve where a word or phrase has been placed between 'to' and the verb: *to actually go*. Although some people disapprove, splitting the infinitive can be:

   1 the clearest way of expressing the meaning: *I'd hate to actually see a ghost:* ('actually' here refers to see, which is the speaker's intention). Note that if the infinitive is not split, 'actually' refers to 'hate': *I'd hate actually to see a ghost*.

   2 The most natural order: *I want to really understand Physics*.

spoonful see **-ful**.

spreadsheet *computers* a widely-used type of business program especially for accounting, which allows figures in various columns to be related to each other and makes 'what if' predictions able to be made. See **what if**.

q. square.

square brackets see **brackets**.

sr Senior.

SRN State Registered Nurse.

St. Saint: Strait: Street.

staccato note the spelling; pronounced [stakahto] a musical instruction to the player to play the notes separated clearly from each other, with a stabbing effect: *The catchy staccato tune made me think of a woodpecker tapping at a tree trunk.*

stadium the plural is either **stadia** (from the Latin) or **stadiums**; the second is commoner nowadays. *The sports ground has two stadiums.*

stalactite/stalagmite both are terms for icicle-shaped deposits of calcium carbonate formed by constantly dripping water in caves and rocky places but: a **stalactite** hangs from the roof and a **stalagmite** rises from the ground.

stanch/staunch both mean to prevent a liquid from flowing out, especially blood from a wound: *Before the ambulance came, the driver used his handkerchief to staunch the blood pouring from Tom's nose.*

standard English the type of English considered acceptable and used by the majority of educated speakers of the language. As there is no rigid set of rules, people often refer to certain varieties as models of correct English, but there is no strict agreement as to what they consist of or which is to be recommended. See **BBC English, Oxford English, Queen's English.**

star wars a widely-used informal name for the strategic defence initiative begun in the USA to develop research into a defence system in outer space as a shield against missile attacks.

stationary/stationery: stationary not moving: *Do not get off the bus unless it is stationary.* **stationery** envelopes and paper etc: *Gifts of stationery are appreciated by people who write a lot.*

statistics see **-ics.**

status pronounced [staytus]: *As a local doctor Robert was conscious that his status made people listen to his opinions.*

staunch see **stanch.**

STD subscriber trunk dialling, making telephone calls by dialling the number without the help of an operator.

step-brother/-sister/half-brother/-sister: step-brother/-sister a child of one's **step-mother** or **-father**, ie the person one of one's parents has married after the death or divorce of the other. *When my father married Mary, Anna became our step-sister.* **half-brother/-sister** the child of one of one's parents and another person: *Fred, my half-brother, was born after Mother divorced my father and married Gerald.*

sterilization see **vasectomy.**

stiletto note the spelling: *stiletto heels are no longer in fashion.*

stimulant/stimulating/stimulus: **stimulant** something such as a drug which helps to make one more active for a time: *Tea and coffee are both stimulants.*

stimulating making more active or lively. *A cold shower has a stimulating effect. I found her lecture very stimulating.* **stimulus** something which acts as a boost to something else: *The government could reduce rates on factory sites as a stimulus to industry in the north.*

stocks and shares/securities are all shares sold to investors so that a public or private organization can raise money for its business and the investor can receive part of the profits, but:

securities is the general name for all such units.

stocks generally refer to securities which pay a fixed rate of interest.

shares are units issued in specific amounts such as £1 or £5; two main types of shares are **preference shares** which earn a fixed annual rate of interest and **ordinary shares** which earn for the holder a share of the profits after the preference shareholders have been paid.

stockbroker a person who buys and sells stocks and shares on the **stock exchange** for other people or organizations.

stock exchange or **stock market** a place where stocks and shares are bought and sold; the business carried on there: *The news of war in oil-producing countries always affects prices on the stock exchange.*

stout see **ale**.

sty/stye: sty 1 a place where a pig is kept, a pigsty. **2** also spelt **stye** an infected swelling on the eyelid.

sub- used with other words to mean under: *submarine; subway.*

subconscious/unconscious both words are used in psychology to refer to the activities of the mind which people are not aware of unless they are brought to their conscious notice by a psychologist or psychiatrist; **subconscious** is commoner: *Dr Furtwengler helped Cyril to conquer his subconscious fear of failure.*

subject/object *grammar* **subject** refers to a noun or pronoun which does the action of the verb; **object** refers to a noun or pronoun which is affected by a verb or preposition. In the sentence *The ball hit the wall, The ball* is the subject, *the wall* the object. In the phrase *on the wall, the wall* is the object of *on.*

suffix a word or syllable added to the end of a word to form a new word: *-able* = capable of being: *enjoyable; -dom* = the condition of, the state of: *boredom; martyrdom.* Compare **prefix**.

super- used with other words to mean above, over; more or bigger than normal: *superstructure; superior; supermarket.*

superior is followed by **to**: *Leather is superior to plastic as a shoe material.*

superlative adjective see **adjective**.

supersede note the spelling. *Typewriters have almost*

been superseded by wordprocessors.

surname see **family name**.

surrender value a term used in insurance for the amount of money which an insured person will receive on his life insurance policy if he cashes it in before the agreed date.

surrogate mother a woman paid to bear a child for a woman who cannot have children. The surrogate is fertilized by sperm taken from the husband of the infertile woman, goes through the pregnancy and hands over the child when it is born.

surveillance pronounced [survaylance]: *Once they suspected Beggs of spying, they kept him under close surveillance, even watching him at night.*

swap/swop both are correct: *Tom swapped his old car for a van which was more useful for his job.*

swat/swot: swat to hit flies etc: *We spent the summer evenings swatting mosquitoes.* **swot** an informal word meaning to study: *Most students start to swot the night before the exam.*

swell past participle **swelled** or **swollen**: *Her ankle has swelled (or swollen) badly.*

syndrome 1 a set of symptoms which, when they appear together, are symptoms of a particular disease: *We know the common cold syndrome: aching head, running nose and a temperature.* 2 a typical set of signs that indicate a certain problem: *Broken home...*

unemployment and poverty are factors in the teenage crime syndrome.

syntax the rules for arranging or combining words in sentences: *The rules of English syntax make it unacceptable to say 'Could please I a cup of coffee have?'*

systems analysis the investigation of methods in an industrial or technical process to improve efficiency by the introduction of new technology, particularly computers. **systems analyst** a person whose job it is to carry out such an operation.

T

tariff note the spelling: **1** a tax put by the government usually on goods coming into a country: *There are high tariffs on the import of certain goods.* **2** a charge for a service: *The tariff for domestic gas has doubled in the last few years.*

tax avoidance/tax evasion: tax avoidance using legal ways of not paying any more tax than is necessary. **tax evasion** using illegal ways of not paying tax. *For the purpose of tax evasion, Denzil put his money in a Hong Kong bank under an assumed name.*

TB tuberculosis.

teetotaller note the spelling.

tele- used with other words to mean **1** at a distance: *telephoto lens* (one which can take photographs from a distance); **2** by television: *telenews.*

tel. telephone.

temp. temperature: temporary.

tense the form of a verb which shows whether it refers to the present, past or future:
    present tense *Today is my birthday.*
    past tense *Yesterday was my birthday.*
    future tense *Tomorrow will be my birthday.*

erm assurance a type of insurance which provides a lump sum for the heirs of an insured person if he dies within a specified period.

erminus/terminal both words are used for the end of a travel route but: **terminus** (plural **terminuses** or **termini**) is commoner for buses and trains and **terminal** for planes; it is also used for the place in a town where buses arrive from the airport.

st-tube baby a popular term for a child born by means of artificial fertilization when a human embryo is produced in a laboratory and transferred to the mother's womb.

stament a will. See **will**.

an Which pronoun should follow **than** in comparisons? *My father is fatter than I* or *My father is fatter then me?* **than I** is more grammatical but **than me** is completely acceptable except in very formal speech. Occasionally, this could cause misunderstandings: *They knew her better than me* needs to be expanded to: *They knew her better than I did.*

an what means than the thing which: *We know nothing more than what the government chooses to tell us.* It is not acceptable to use **than what** to mean than: *'I speak English better than what some people do,'* he growled in his uncouth way.

at/which/who pronouns which relate or link part of a sentence to a previous noun or pronoun: *The comic that I used to read was the Beano. She knew a man who had six wives. Animals which hunt in packs are dangerous.* In all cases, **that** can be used instead of **who** or **which**.

their/them/they: are used to refer to an indefinite person who sex is not specified: *If anyone needs me they can leave their phone number and I will contact them.* The alternative is to use **he/him/his**, but this is very formal.

their/there: **their** belonging to or connected with them: *their houses.* **there** in, to, at that place: *They live there in the castle on that cliff.*

third party a type of insurance which only covers a driver for claims made against him by another person for injury and legal costs for damage which he may have caused. It does not cover him for similar damage to himself or his own vehicle. **third party fire and theft** covers the driver for the above and for damage to his own vehicle by fire and theft.

third person the grammatical forms of pronouns and verbs when they refer to neither the speaker nor the person being spoken to, eg *he, it, them* are third person pronouns: *Mothers often talk to babies in the third person — 'Mummy's cross with baby, isn't she*

Third World: 1 those countries in Africa, Asia and Latin America which belong politically to neither the Communist nor the Capitalist block, but form an unaligned group. **2** all the underdeveloped countries in the world.

tilde the mark ~ used for example above an *n* in Spanish to show the pronunciation: *mañana* pronounced [manyana], meaning tomorrow.

time-sharing 1 ownership of a share in a holiday home through a company which arranges for each part-owner to use the accommodation for a certain period of the year. **2** *computers* a system by which two or more users can use a computer at the same time but for different purposes.

tire see **tyre**.

titles and forms of address see **letters**.

titles of work etc titles of the following are usually printed in italics, with a capital letter at the beginning of each important word; when typed or handwritten, the titles are underlined: books, magazines, plays, films, newspapers, long poems, pieces of music, paintings etc.

Inverted commas are used for: (short) poems, songs, articles in books or magazines.

The first chapter of *Household Hints* is entitled 'How to cope with a domestic crisis'.

title deeds legal documents which prove that a person is the owner of property or land.

TM abbreviation of **transcendental meditation**, a technique originating in Hinduism of arriving, by means of deep concentrated thought, at a calm and enlightened mental state which is beyond normal human experience.

ton/tonne: ton a measurement in weight of 2 240

pounds (**long ton**, the equivalent of 1 016 kilograms or 2 000 pounds (**short ton**, the equivalent of 9 07? kilograms). Note that the first is more commonly used in the UK and the second in the USA. **tonne** a metric weight of 1 000 kilograms (the equivalent of 2 20? pounds).

tonsillitis note the spelling.

tornado plural **tornados**.

torpedo plural **torpedoes**: *As they returned across the Atlantic the ship was hit by several torpedoes.*

Tory see **Conservative**.

toward/towards are both correct; **towards** is commoner in British and **toward** in American English.

toxic/toxaemic: **toxic** of poisonous substances, poisonous: *These soaps contain no toxic materials* **toxaemic**, also spelt **toxemic**, suffering from **toxaemia**, a medical condition in which there i poison in the bloodstream: *On admission to hospita he was found to be in a toxaemic state.*

trade union/trades union both forms are acceptable but the first is commoner except in the name **Trade Union Congress**, now usually referred to as the **TUC**

trait pronounced [tray] or [trate]: *Maggie has man traits of character which people find irritating.*

tranquillize/tranquillizer note the spelling: *The war air had a tranquillizing effect on the normall boisterous children. He has been on tranquillizers fo* *a week and walks around like a zombie.*

trans- used with other words to mean across: *transfusion; Trans-Siberian Railway.*

transcendental meditation see **TM**.

trauma pronounced [**trawma**] or [**trowma**], plural **traumata** or **traumas** but the first is used mainly in medical language. **1** a bad shock which may do serious psychological damage: *The trauma caused by being abandoned as a child affected Muriel all her life.* **2** any serious wound or injury.

The adjective is **traumatic** and is now also used of anything shocking or deeply upsetting: *The effects of the works closure on the economy of the town were traumatic.*

treble/triple as verbs are interchangeable, though **treble** is commoner: *Rich Uncle Humphrey has trebled (tripled) my allowance.* As adjectives, however: **triple** describes something which has three sections or aspects: *The tank has a triple lining for safety.* **treble** means multiplied by three: *Nick scored a treble win on the football pools.*

tree diagram see **decision tree**.

tribunal a special type of court set up to deal with a particular kind of problem: *Harriet went to the rent tribunal because the landlord charged too much for her flat.*

truly: Yours truly see **letters**.

trustee see **will**.

TT teetotal; of cattle etc, tuberculin-tested (ie free of certain diseases).

TUC see **trade union**.

turf plural **turfs** or **turves**.

turnover in business, the total amount of money which comes in during a certain period: *They have a turnover of £1 million per year with a profit of £50 000.*

turquoise there are two pronunciations [**turkwoyz**] [**turkwaz**] a blue-green semi-precious stone.

turtle *computer* 1 a small robot used mainly in primary education which can be instructed in LOGO (see **LOGO**) to move around the room and draw or write on paper, or a similar device on the screen shaped like an arrowhead which can be instructed by the computer to produce graphics.

TV television.

typewritten letter see **letters**.

tyre/tire: tyre is used in British English, tire in American.

U

UFO unidentified flying object.

UHF ultra-high frequency.

UK United Kingdom (of Great Britain and Northern Ireland). See **Britain**.

ultimatum plural **ultimatums** or **ultimata**; the second is rather formal: *The manager gave one of the customers no less than five warnings before the ultimatum that he would prosecute if they did not pay all the debts in full.*

ultra- used with other words to mean beyond (the limits of): *ultrasonic* (beyond the limit of human hearing).

umlaut a symbol to indicate the pronunciation of certain vowels in German: *Zürich.* Compare **diaerisis.**

UN United Nations.

unaware/unawares The adjective is always **unaware**: *The smuggler unloaded the drugs unaware that the police were waiting to pounce on him.* The adverb is **unawares** or **unaware**: *The earthquake caught everyone unawares (unaware) and panic broke out.*

underlining see **titles of works etc.**

UNESCO United Nations Educational, Scientific and Cultural Organization.

unexceptionable/unexceptional: **unexceptionable** adequate, giving no cause for complaint: *Her remarks at the meeting were quite unexceptionable, but her behaviour provoked a lot of adverse comment.* **unexceptional** not specially good or worthy of praise: *To our disappointment the luxury hotel was unexceptional and similar to some modest establishments.*

UNICEF United Nations Children's Fund.

unilateral refers to an action taken by one group without consulting others who they would normally come to an agreement with first: *unilateral disarmament.*

uninterested see **disinterested**.

unique the only one of its kind, having no rival or equal: *The six-legged tiger at the circus was claimed to be unique.* Note that *quite, most unique* are not logical.

unisex applicable to or used by both sexes: *Many women's hairdresser's have become unisex salons and welcome male clients.*

United Kingdom see **Britain**.

United States of America see **America**.

unit trust an organization for the collective buying of shares so that each shareholder who buys a number of units has its risks spread over a wide range of investments; also used to refer to one of these units: *I've just bought a lot of unit trusts.*

UN(O) United Nations (Organization).

unreadable see **illegible**.

upon/on in most sentences, **upon** can be used instead of **on**, but it is now considered rather old-fashioned or literary: *Robert mused upon the memories of his childhood.*

uptight 1 tense, anxious: *Fergus gets very uptight when he has to speak in public.* **2** stiff, formal, unable to relax with other people: *Jill's parents are so uptight that we can't drop in on them without arranging beforehand.*

upward/upwards *adjective* **upward**: *an upward trend in expenditure.* *adverb* **upward** and **upwards** are both correct: *The climbers crawled slowly upward (upwards) against the wind.*

urban/urbane: urban to do with a city: *In nineteenth-century England the urban populations increased dramatically, especially in Manchester and Liverpool.* **urbane** sophisticated, refined: *John F Kennedy charmed people with his urbane manner and good looks.*

US United States.

USA United States of America: United States Army.

USAF United States Air Force.

use/usage are both concerned with using things but: **use** refers to the practice of using: *The use of wordprocessors is increasing rapidly.* **usage** refers to particular ways of using, especially language:

Goodday is old-fashioned in Engand, but in Australian usage it is a normal form of greeting.

used to the negative forms are: **1** formal: *I used not to smoke.* (shortened to: *I usedn't to smoke.*) **2** less formal: *I didn't use to smoke.* The question forms are: **1** formal: *Used I to annoy you?* **2** less formal: *Did I use to annoy to you?*

user-friendly *computers* decribes something to do with a computer, usually a program, which is easy to understand and use.

USN United States Navy.

USS United States Ship/Steamer.

USSR Union of Soviet Socialist Republics.

V volts.

v versus, against; see (in Latin *vide*); verse.

vacation 1 in British English, a period when universities, colleges, schools and law courts are on holiday. *Many university students find temporary work in the vacation.* **2** in American English, a holiday period. **3** leaving a place free of people: *The hotel manager insisted on vacation of the rooms by 10 a.m. on the day of departure.*

vagina pronounced [vajinea].

vain/vane/vein: vain describes a person who is too proud of him- or herself: *It was very vain of Oliver to think he knew more than his father.* **vane** a flat blade specially shaped to turn easily in the wind: *the vanes of a windmill; a weather vane.* **vein** see **artery**.

valuable see **invaluable**.

value-added tax see **VAT**.

vasectomy/sterilization operations which make a person unable to have children. **vasectomy** is the operation for male sterilization, involving the cutting of the *vas deferens* just below the skin of the groin. **sterilization** usually refers to the various types of operation to make a woman sterile.

VAT pronounced [vee ay tee] or [vat] abbreviation for **value-added tax**, a tax added to the price of an article when it is sold and to the cost of services performed.

VC Victoria Cross.

VD abbreviation for **venereal disease**, a disease which is passed on to other people by sexual activity.

VDU *computers* abbreviation for **visual display unit**, a television-like screen or monitor. See also **monitor**.

vegan/vegetarian neither of them eats meat or fish, but a **vegan** does not eat animal products such as eggs, cheese and milk either.

vein see **artery**.

verb a word which refers to being, eg *was*, or happening or doing, eg *escaped*: *Mactavish was delighted when he escaped from prison.*

venereal disease see **VD**.

vengeance see **avenge**.

VHF very high frequency.

via 1 by way of (a place): *We went to London via Oxford.* 2 used only in informal English, by means of: *He learnt English via the World Service of the BBC. She came into computing via teaching.*

vicar see **rector**.

victuals pronounced [**vittles**]: *The pirates on the Mermaid always referred to their dried fish and ship's biscuits as victuals.*

VIP Very Important Person.

visual display unit see VDU.

viz namely (in Latin *videlicet*).

vol volume.

vs versus, against.

VSO Voluntary Service Overseas.

voluntarily pronounced [**voluntrily**]: *Without any prompting Nicholas gave up his room voluntarily to the refugees.*

W

was/were see if/were.

wave 1 to move freely to and fro: *The flags waved in the wind.* **2** to form a curved shape: *Granny used to wave her hair by plaiting it at night.*

    waive 1 to give up something one has a right to: *Lord Sump kindly waived his fee and gave us a lecture free of charge.* **2** not to force someone to pay a fee, a fine or obey a law as they ought to: *As the man in the dock was old and crippled, the judge waived the usual £50 fine.*

WC water closet.

we has several functions: **1** the first person plural (see **first person**): *We are all brothers.* **2** the royal plural used in former times by the monarch instead of I: *Queen Victoria replied to her minister, 'We are not amused'.* **3** as an impersonal pronoun to make statements sound less arrogant, dogmatic etc: *'We have seen how the television news has given a one-sided view,' said the minister.*

Welsh see **Celtic**.

Welsh rarebit/Welsh rabbit both names are used for a dish of melted cheese (sometimes with other things added), served on hot buttered toast.

west see **north**.

wet *verb* the past is **wetted** or **wet**: *They wetted the surface to test it. Little Jimmy wet the bed again last night. adjective: slang, in politics* describes a member of right-wing group or party who is considered by colleagues to have left-wing tendencies. Also used as a noun: *The wets wanted more money for OAPs.*

wharf both **wharfs** and **wharves** are correct plurals. *The wharves along the Thames are no longer used for commercial shipping, but yachts are moored there now.*

what/which both are used to ask about a choice but: **what** is used when there is unlimited choice: *What presents did you get for Christmas?* **which** is used when the choice is clearly limited: *Which twin plays tennis?* (which of the twins).

what if' predictions *computers* a way of making financial forecasts by means of a spreadsheet, particularly in business finance. See **spreadsheet**.

which see **what** and **that**.

while/whilst both are correct.

whisky/whiskey: **whisky** is the spelling used for the spirit distilled in Scotland, also known as **Scotch whisky** or **Scotch**, while **whiskey** is made in both Ireland and America.

WHO World Health Organization.

who see **that**.

who/whom: **who** is the subject pronoun (like

I/he/they etc): *Who wrote this play?* **whom** is the object pronoun like (*me/him/them*): *By whom wa. this play written?* **whom** is still in use, but the majority of speakers find **who** more acceptable: *Wh. was this play written by?*

will see **shall**.

will a legal document in which a person sets out how h or she wants his or her property to be dealt with afte death. Although it is best when possible to ask lawyer to prepare the document, a legally-binding wi can be written without a lawyer if certain rules ar followed:

   1 It is necessary to appoint one or two executor whose job is to see that the will is carried out. A ban or solicitor can act as executor or any person ove eighteen, including someone who actually benefi from the will.

   2 Two witnesses must be present to sign that th person making the will actually signed it in th presence of both witnesses. The witnesses must people who do not benefit from the will.

   3 An attestation clause must be included in the w to confirm that the will was signed and witness correctly: *Signed by X in our presence and by us his/hers.*

   4 It is advisable, although not absolutely necessa to include the date when the will was signed and al the addresses and occupations of the witnesses.

   5 Any previous will must be revoked (cancelled

An example of a will might be:

Will of John Aker of 3 Oak Gardens, Tamworth, Staffordshire

I revoke previous wills. I appoint my sister Delia Aker of 2 Park Court, Tamworth, Staffordshire to be the sole executor of this will and leave to her everything I own.

Date: 19 March 1987

Signature: John Aker

Signed by John Aker in our presence and by us in his.

Sandra Laker	Hilda Lord
The Elms	1 Bell Rd
Stone	Madely
Staffs	Staffs
Dentist	Florist

Note that if a person wishes to alter any part of the will, or to add something to it, he or she must make a **codicil**, which is a legally-acceptable method. It must be signed and witnessed in exactly the same way as a will, but the witnesses do not need to be the same as the two who signed the original will. There is no limit to the number of codicils which can be made, but sometimes it may be more convenient to make a new will.

Example of a codicil:

This is the first codicil to the will, dated 19 March 1987, of me, John Aker of 3 Oak Gardens, Tamworth, Staffs.

1 I give to nephew Christopher Moore any books or paintings acquired by me after 1 April 1987.

2 In all other respects, I confirm my will.

Date: 6 October 1987.
Signature: John Aker.

Signed by John Aker in our presence and by us in his

Breta Chekes	Michael Eccles
5 Roman Way	43 Merrills Road
Bromsgrove	Didsbury
Birmingham	Manchester
Nurse	Lecturer

windward see **leeward**.

woollen note the spelling.

wordprocessor an arrangement on a computer or separate machine which allows the user to type a text, eg a letter, onto the screen and correct or alter it if necessary, before printing the whole text on a printer.

would see **should**.

wrath pronounced [roth] in British English, [rath] in American English: *The natives thought that God was angry with them and the thunder was a sign of his wrath.*

XYZ

x pronounced [z] at the beginning of a word: *xerox* [zeroks].

ye 1 this is a mistaken form of *the*: *ye old inn*. The initial letter is not *Y* but was originally a letter thorn which represented *th* and looked in some scripts like the letter *Y*. **2** an older form of **you** plural: *Ye gods!* **3** a dialect form of **you** singular: *Bless ye, child!*

yes there are two ways to punctuate *yes* when it is quoted: *When I asked her permission, she said yes. When I asked her permission, she said, 'Yes'.*

YHA Youth Hostels Association.

YMCA Young Men's Christian Association.

Yn Yen.

yoga/yogi: yoga a Hindu system of philosophy aiming to free the self and unite it with the universe, using complicated physical and mental exercises. **yogi** a person who is skilled in yoga, especially an advanced teacher of it.

yoghurt, yogurt, yoghourt all three spellings are acceptable.

yolk/yoke: yoke the yellow substance containing protein and fat inside an egg. **yoke 1** a device for linking two animals together at the neck so that they can work as a team. **2** oppression or slavery: *The slaves groaned under the tyrant's yoke.*

yomp in informal English, to march across rough country, usually used of soldiers: *Luckily the marines were suitably dressed for yomping across the moors in pouring rain.*

you 1 the second person pronoun — see **second person**. **2** an impersonal pronoun — see **one**.

you know/you see frequently-used fillers in conversation which some people object to when they are used too often: *You know, I'd rather you didn't hitchhike to Spain. It's quite dangerous, you see.*
If not over-used, however, they have valuable uses:
   1 they give the speaker time to reorganize his words.
   2 they keep friendly contact open even when there is nothing special to say.
   3 they can soften the effect of a harsh message: *Father had to punish you, you know.*

your/yours/you're: your/yours belonging to you (Note that it is not possible to have an apostrophe in this word): *This is your cake. It's yours.* **you're** abbreviation for **you are**: *You're very kind.*

Yours faithfully, Yours sincerely, Yours truly see **letters**.

Yr year.

yuppy abbreviation for young upwardly mobile person

refers to a clever young person, especially one working in the City of London, who earns a very high salary.

YWCA Young Women's Christian Association.

z the name of this letter is **zed** in British English and **zee** in American.